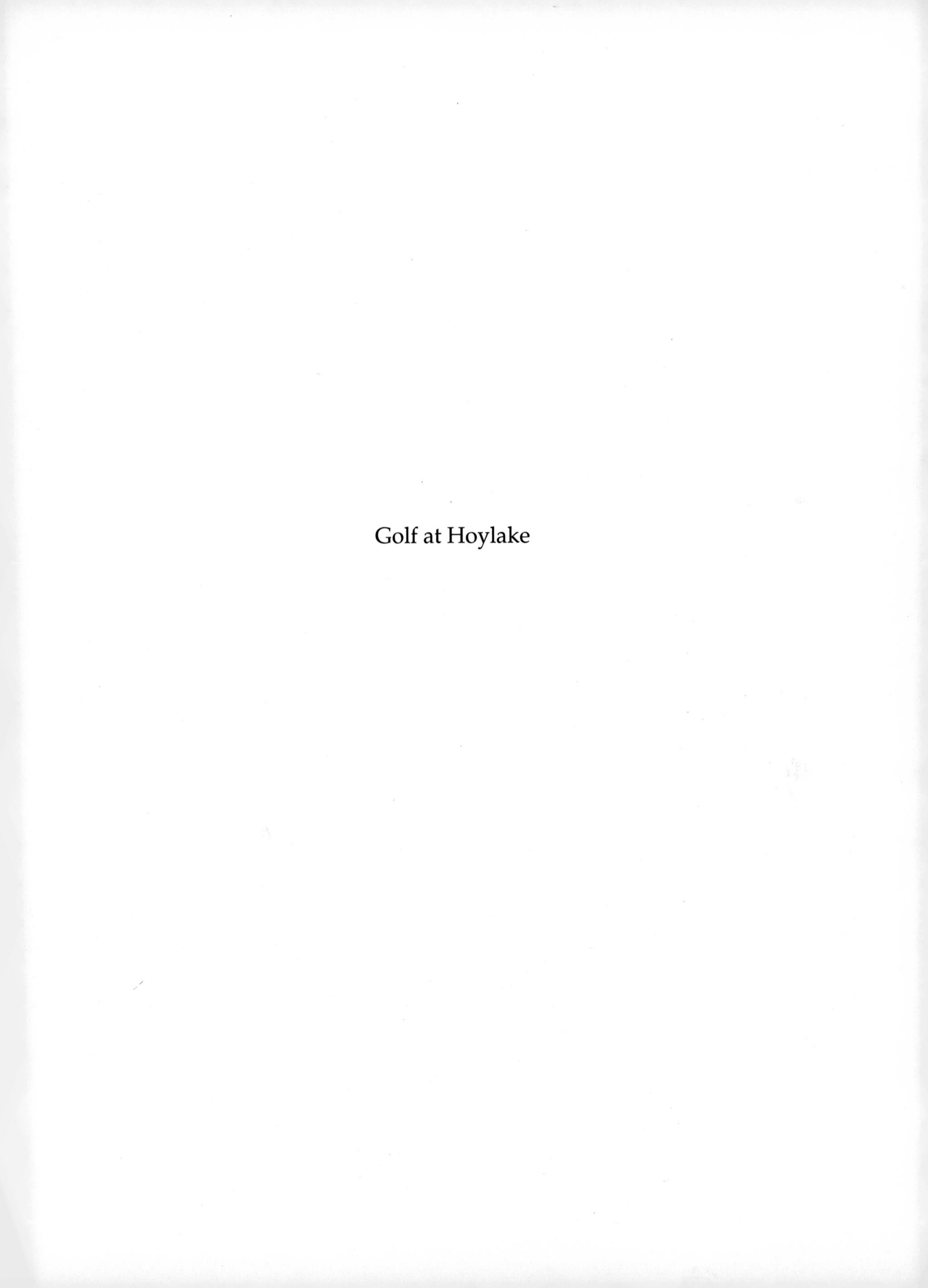

Golf at Hoylake

To Nigel,

With much love

from

Roger & Wendy

Christmas 1990.

The Hoylake Triumvirate

Jack Graham Harold Hilton John Ball

Golf at Hoylake

A Royal Liverpool Golf Club Anthology

Compiled and Arranged
by

John Behrend

John Graham

Grant Books, Worcestershire
1990

ISBN 0 907186 12 2

Typeset by Severnside Printers Limited

Published for Royal Liverpool Golf Club
by

GH
Grant Hobbs

Grant Books
Victoria Square, Droitwich,
Worcestershire
WR9 8DE

Published by
Grant Books
for
Royal Liverpool Golf Club
in a limited edition of
1125 copies of which 125 are presentation copies

This copy No.
233

John
Behrend

John
Graham

Contents

Acknowledgements

There are many people to thank both for the content and the production of this anthology.

Golf is fortunate to have so many gifted authors both ancient and modern. The task, which compilers of an anthology must undertake, of delving into their writings, has been one of the pleasures. Our thanks firstly go to them, not just for the chapters and articles that have been chosen and which have been fully acknowledged at the end of each section, but for encouraging us to discover or read again some of the other accounts of great golfing occasions. As one might expect, Bernard Darwin figures prominently. For these extracts acknowledgement is made for the permission of A.P. Watt Ltd, on behalf of Ursula Mommens, Lady Darwin and Paul Ashton.

Secondly our thanks are due to our fellow amateurs — members of the Club who have researched and written several of the articles. We have a feeling that they too have enjoyed doing it. Pen pictures of these contributors are at the end of the book. In amongst this group is one who is by no means an amateur, Leslie Edwards. Our very special thanks go to him not just for what he has written, but for his memories, his help with illustrations and his general encouragement. Mention should also be made of Edward Birchall who more than twenty years ago embarked on the task of updating the Golf Club history. Sadly only a few chapters had emerged when he died. It is only proper that his literary skills should find a place in this anthology and we have selected his account of the 1936 Open for inclusion.

Thanks also are due to John Pugh, who has cheerfully undertaken the laborious task of copy editing, and to Audrey Ellison who has typed and retyped many of the articles.

The illustrations have been drawn mostly from Club sources. There is one Club source that gives endless pleasure — the pen and brush of Jos Armitage. You will read about him later in this book, but his line drawings at the end of each section are specially appreciated. One or two other illustrations are from more recent books or magazines; an acknowledgement, where possible, has been made.

Every effort has been made to contact copyright holders of both articles and illustrations, though in some cases, where there has been no response, we have assumed that "no news is good news". We apologise for any indiscretion.

Introduction

Golf Club centenaries have been coming thick and fast. To mark such occasions it is not unusual for a Club history to be produced. The Royal Liverpool 1988 Captain, Nicko Williams, attended a number of centenary celebrations, enjoying the golfing and social programme to the full, and often returning with a gift of such a book, elegantly presented and put together with loving care by some senior member of the Club.

Our Club was founded 120 years ago, which is not a very significant number, but that did not deter Nicko, with his infectious enthusiasm, from proposing that our history should be updated. It is more than fifty years since *The Royal Liverpool Golf Club* by Guy B. Farrar was produced, although for our centenary Leslie Edwards wrote an accomplished booklet with a couple of dozen pages which was served up to members and guests with the smoked salmon at the celebration dinner. Subsequently this was updated by John Brocklehurst for our overseas visitors to the Walker Cup in 1983.

The Club owes much to Tom Potter and the early Secretaries for leaving us the material for such books. But it was Guy Farrar with all his painstaking research and his easy style of writing who did the hard work. His book is now a collector's item, and when from time to time one appears for sale in an antiquarian bookseller's catalogue or at auction the asking price is about £200. Those of us who have a copy treasure it. To update such a book would just not be possible, but from Nicko's decree the seeds of an anthology were sown.

Guy Farrar, the son of one of Hoylake's early members, was not only a fine golfer, who competed in the Championships and picked up half-a-dozen Scratch medals, but was also a good judge of golfers and golfing matters. This he demonstrated when he was Secretary between 1944 and 1957. During this period he set high standards for the Club and the links, but in common with many bachelors, he was a shy and reserved person. To new members and visitors he appeared intimidating, but underneath this daunting veneer was a wise and kindly man. He made his mark also as a writer and a photographer in the 1930s. He wrote a weekly golfing column for the *Liverpool Daily Post* under the pseudonym of Calamity Jane. As a photographer he was Chairman of the local photographic society and was noted for his ornithological studies and for his detail of the interior of churches and cathedrals. Pat Healey, a member of the society, remembers him in his own dark room, whilst stressing the importance of total cleanliness, leaning over a tray of developing solution with half an inch of ash on the end of his cigarette. In truth that is how most of us remember him, and perhaps for his nasally mumbled remarks (it is difficult to talk any other way with a cigarette in one's mouth). In my case these remarks were often humorous and always friendly, but that was not always so. Richard Cornelius tells of the time that he holed the 10th in 2, with Guy watching from the 11th tee. As he walked towards him expecting some congratulatory noise, he got instead "I still don't like your style." When the daffodils between the 1st tee and 16th green first sprang to life, Alex Warnock commented to Guy on how nice it would be to see more colour, bushes and shrubs perhaps, around the course; the curt answer came "People don't come to Hoylake for fun." On another occasion he was asked why the flag was not at half mast to mark the funeral of a departed member. "He hadn't paid his subscription" was the reply. Of one thing one can have no doubt — that Guy Farrar had a deep knowledge of, interest in, and affection for the Royal Liverpool Golf Club, and the Club could not have had a finer chronicler.

Your humble chroniclers of today share the same interest and affection, and that is not a bad starting point for collaborating on a book about the Club.

What is special about Hoylake? In simple terms, it is the links and its history — the famous players and the great Championships. It has therefore been easy to decide on a basic shape for the anthology. The first requirement was to find articles about how golf started at Hoylake, the first lay-out and the evolvement of the links that we now know. In the last 60 years there have been few major changes, but before 1930 there was constant experiment and alteration. Valley, Kirby, Warren, and Football Field were all names of early Hoylake holes. They, like some of nature's original bunkers — Dun's Grave, Hell, and Inkpot, have all disappeared. Although the pages that follow will not illuminate the reader on their whereabouts, hopefully they will at least help to preserve the names and the stories of the existing holes.

The second section covers the ten Open Championships and sixteen Amateurs which have been held at Hoylake; there have been countless other events — Professional, Amateur, Ladies, International matches, County championships, University matches. Scarcely a year goes by without an event of sufficient importance to bring the golfing press to Hoylake, and many million words have been written by these illustrious golfing scribes. One cannot pretend to have read more than a few thousands of them. The task of selection has been made somewhat easier by the fact that five of the Open Champions have written autobiographies, including in them accounts of their victories, and there is no better view of a Championship than from the horse's mouth.

Hoylake has had its share of heroes and characters, so the third section covers a dozen or so of Hoylake's best. If the emphasis is on the past more than the present that is not unnatural. We have been a bit short of Open and Amateur Champions these last fifty years!

One of the great pleasures we have had in compiling this anthology has been talking to members, or listening to them talk, particularly the older ones who have so many memories of strange and amusing happenings. Some of these have found their way into the articles in the first three sections. The fourth section is wide-ranging, largely written by members of the Club, and has given an opportunity for some more of these incidents to be recorded. There is one that we heard only the other day, and we hope Betty Lloyd, who has written a delightful article about Gladys Ravenscroft, will forgive us for poaching it for this Introduction. Gladys, a girl of ample proportions, was taught the fundamentals of her golf swing by the great Fred Robson, who was for a time Professional at Bromborough. He was becoming somewhat exasperated as she hit shot after shot over the top. "It's no good Miss Ravenscroft. You've just got to get your 'bussies' out of the way of your 'wrissies'" he said.

I hope our readers will get as much enjoyment from what follows as we have had in putting it together.

Early History and the Links

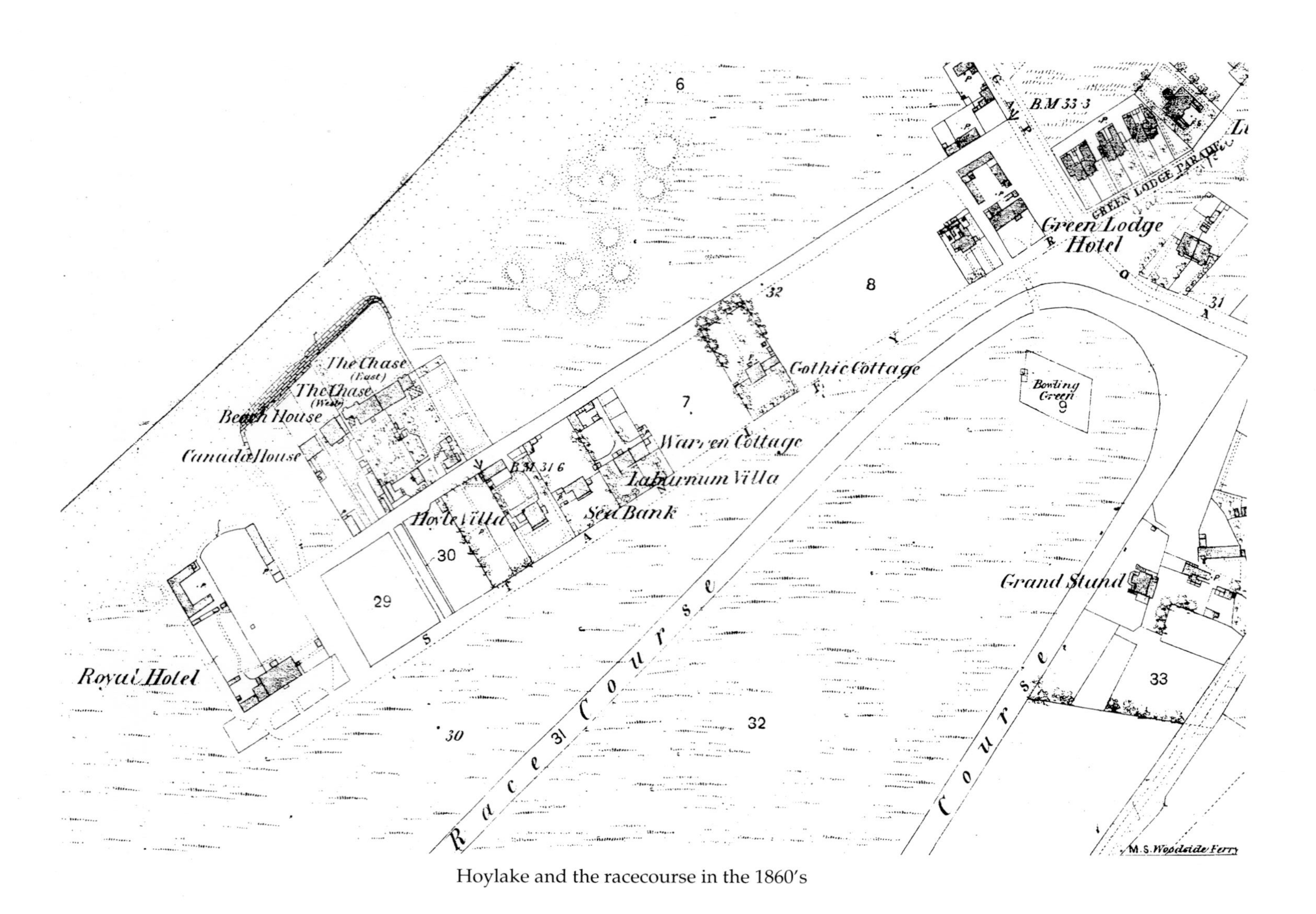

Hoylake and the racecourse in the 1860's

Early Days

Bernard Darwin

The Hoylake of to-day is populous and flourishing. Save only on the sandhills, where they look across to Wales, rows of houses stretch along the edges of the links. The links itself, which has been the breeding-ground of champions, is generally recognized as the finest golf course in Britain. The Hoylake of 1869, the year in which golf first came to rouse it from its pleasant drowsiness, was a very different place. Let us imagine ourselves sitting on the grass, where now is the club house. What should we have seen? Over against us there would have been the Royal Hotel, without the club rooms that were afterwards added. It must have been much as it was when Miss Anna Seward, the "Swan of Lichfield", came to stay there instead of at Weymouth, admired the lovely "downs" and the bathing that was so good for "cowardly bathers" and wrote in its praise some of the worst poetry ever perpetrated even by an eighteenth-century poetess. To the right of the Royal would have been two houses, Chase East and Chase West, which are still there; farther to the right again one or two cottages. There would have been no other human habitation to be seen, and at our backs fields would have stretched unbroken as far as West Kirby. Between us and the Royal there would have been the posts of the racecourse making a circuit round what is now the practising ground called "The Field". To-day only two of those posts survive, sacred and battered relics of the past, on the verge of the fairway going to the Home hole. Finally, where there is now a row of gardens, there would have been the quaint little grand stand.

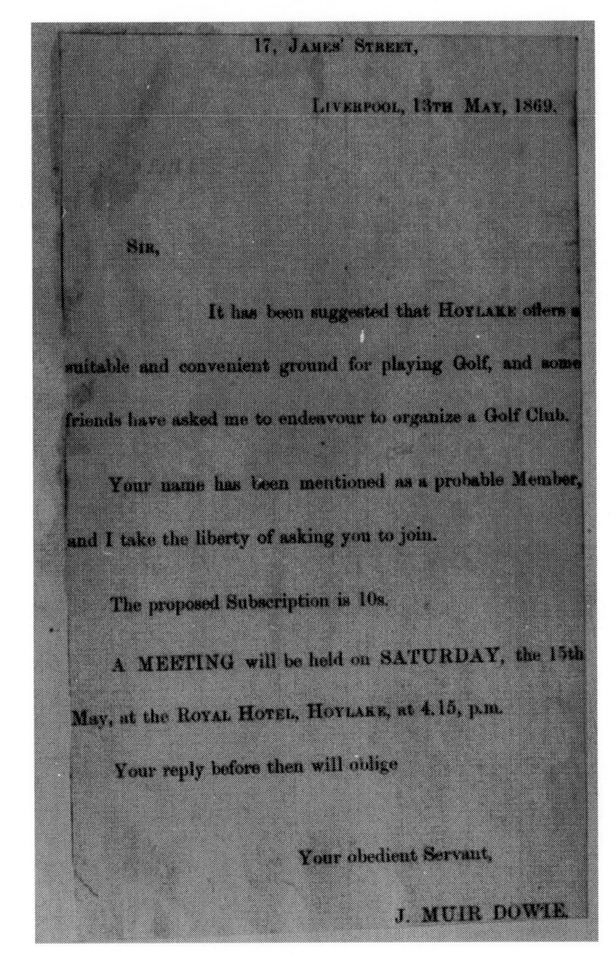

17, James' Street,

Liverpool, 13th May, 1869.

Sir,

It has been suggested that Hoylake offers a suitable and convenient ground for playing Golf, and some friends have asked me to endeavour to organize a Golf Club.

Your name has been mentioned as a probable Member, and I take the liberty of asking you to join.

The proposed Subscription is 10s.

A MEETING will be held on SATURDAY, the 15th May, at the Royal Hotel, Hoylake, at 4.15, p.m.

Your reply before then will oblige

Your obedient Servant,

J. MUIR DOWIE.

Notice of the first meeting

Twice a year, on the occasion of the races, Hoylake presumably became a gay spot. Otherwise the rabbits must have had it largely to themselves except for those who came sometimes to shoot them. I like the picture drawn for me by Jack Morris of himself and old Mr. John Ball standing at the door of the Royal. I call him "old" to distinguish him from his illustrious son, but he was at that time "Mr. John Ball junr.", and the John of to-day — then in early knicker-bockers — was "tertius". In the distance are seen some people approaching, and they are eagerly scanned. "They don't look much like golfers," says Jack Morris. "Dang it," replies Mr. Ball, "who would come here except to play golf?"

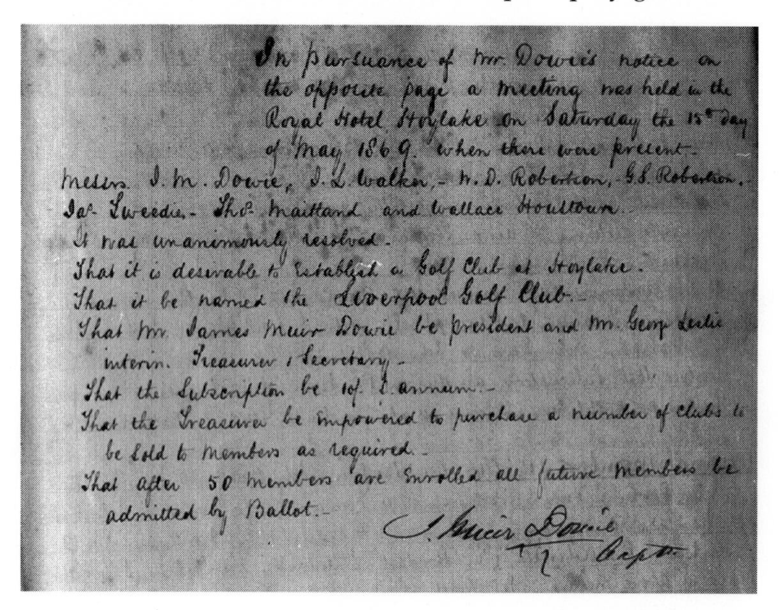

In pursuance of Mr. Dowie's notice on the opposite page a meeting was held in the Royal Hotel Hoylake on Saturday the 15th day of May 1869. when there were present.
Messrs. J. M. Dowie, J. L. Walker, W. D. Robertson, G. S. Robertson, Jas. Tweedie, Thos. Maitland and Wallace Houltoun.
It was unanimously resolved.
That it is desirable to establish a Golf Club at Hoylake.
That it be named the Liverpool Golf Club.
That Mr. James Muir Dowie be president and Mr. Geo. Leslie interim Treasurer & Secretary.
That the Subscription be 10/- p. annum.
That the Treasurer be empowered to purchase a number of clubs to be sold to members as required.
That after 50 members are enrolled all future members be admitted by Ballot.
J. Muir Dowie
Capt.

The first minute

It was on the 13th of May 1869 that the first step was taken in the golfers' invasion of this sleepy paradise. On that day there was issued from 17 James Street, Liverpool, a circular letter signed "J. Muir Dowie", beginning "Sir, It has been suggested that Hoylake offers a suitable and convenient ground for playing golf and some friends have asked me to endeavour to organize a golf club." The letter went on to say that the proposed subscription was ten shillings a year and that there was to be a meeting at the Royal Hotel on Saturday, 15 May. The

James Muir Dowie

meeting was duly held and seven people attended it, all with good Scottish names — Dowie, Walker, two Robertsons, Tweedie, Maitland, and Houston. Mr. Dowie was elected president, Mr. George Leslie interim treasurer and secretary, and the treasurer was empowered "to purchase a number of clubs to be sold to members as required".

Things now began to move fast. A nine-hole course was laid out by George Morris, an elder brother of Old Tom's and the father of Jack, who had migrated from St. Andrews to Carnoustie. On the 2nd June there was notice of a confirmatory meeting to be held on the 5th "when several experienced golfers had promised to attend" and play in matches. The name of Mr. John Ball junr. now appears as a member of the council, and in the list of original members are W. Ball, A. and L. Stoddart (a good Hoylake name), and R. Chambers junr., who was the best amateur of his day in Scotland, and some connexion of the Dowie family. A Liverpool paper gives an account of the proceedings. It appears that there were on the same day some "amateur horse and pony races", but golf on account of its novelty was deemed by the reporter to be the better copy. "The sons of Scotia", he remarked, had often wanted to form a club but had failed "owing to the difficulty of obtaining a suitable 'link' — the technical name for golfing ground". Mr. Robert Chambers and George Morris played the first match and later played in a foursome — Mr. John Dun of Warrington and Morris against Mr. Chambers and Mr. Leslie. This ended in a 'draw', and finally Mr. Chambers played a single with Mr. Dun; he holed out from "behind a low sandbank", and the ladies and gentlemen who watched were highly delighted. The day ended with a "substantial dinner, mine host of the Royal Hotel (himself a convert to the game) exerting himself to the utmost". Mr. Ball, it should here be added, was not only the landlord of the Royal but also a farmer and the tenant of the links, and it was from him that the club held its first lease.

John Ball senior

In the following month the secretary wrote to the members: "I have much pleasure in informing you that Mr. Morris a professional player of ability, has been engaged by the club and is now resident in Hoylake. His time is at the command of members who wish to play ... It is hoped that experienced players will waive rights of precedence of engagement when young players are desirous of instruction." Thus Jack Morris arrived in July 1869 at Hoylake, where he is still, an honoured and beloved institution and a life member of the club. In spite of the enthusiasm of the early members there was in fact very little going on at Hoylake except on a Saturday, and on week-days the links were almost as solitary as before. George Morris brought his son to Hoylake and stayed some days to see him settled in. After being there nearly a week he said, "I see very little doing here. Would you like to come home again with me?", but Jack stoutly declined, as he told me, to "show the white feather so soon". He stayed on, teaching and playing when he was wanted, and occupying his abundant leisure in making balls for some good customers in Scotland. He had a club maker and also got clubs from Tom Morris and Patrick. His workshop was a loose box behind the Royal, and when the time of the races came he had to turn out of it. One of his early jobs was to make a little club for Master John Ball tertius, but that young genius taught himself and had no lessons. As far as the links was concerned there does not seem to have been much to be done, for it was not till several years after Jack's arrival that a putting green was ever rolled or mown: the rabbits did the green keeping. There were no tins in the holes; one of the first set of rules in July 1869 lays down that "No ball shall be teed less than six club lengths nor more that ten lengths from the hole", and when the player wanted sand to make his tee he took it, after the old Scottish fashion, from the bottom of the hole.

The club was called the Liverpool Golf Club, alternative suggestions for names in the form of "Hoylake" and "West Lancashire and Cheshire" being rejected. In 1871, through the good offices of Colonel Kennard, sometime Field Marshal of the Royal Blackheath Club and Hoylake's second captain, Prince Arthur, Duke of Connaught, consented to be honorary president, and the club became Royal accordingly.

(from *Hoylake & West Kirby — A Parochial History* by John Brownbill, published by Henry Young & Sons 1928)

The First Course

Major F. P. Hopkins

Many golfers ask "What are the Hoylake Links like?" The starting point or ninth hole, is a short spoonshot from the hotel, which faces south on to the racecourse, and backs north to the sea of St. George's Channel, or the Liverpool reach of the Mersey. In driving off to the first hole, the rails of the racecourse have to be avoided; the straight line would be to the grandstand, but by keeping to the right a space is found, and rushes and rabbit scrapes avoided. The second drive across the rushes takes one into moderately safe ground within an iron shot of the hole — a mugged stoke is almost sure to bring grief in rush or scrape. The approaches to this green are not easy but the green is good and keen. To the second hole, the line is along the racecourse — straight driving is necessary. On the right are scrapes, on the left, a hedge, in the centre, a rail; keep the line and two drives and a short spoon will put the ball upon the green. The rail throughout is a nuisance — forever getting in the way. The third hole is, at present, rather uncertain from many rabbit holes but the Club are improving the line by filling up the rabbit holes and if the ball lies well two drives will take the ball to the hole; but caution is necessary in approaching this hole, which has a ditch before and behind. It is, however, well placed and requires golf to play it. This hole may be said to be the south-western extremity of the links. The fourth hole points in a northerly direction and is a straight, long hole, with nothing to bring up a moderately straight good driver. There are rushes near the tee and ditches on the course; but three drives and a cleek, or four drives, ought to put the ball within putting distance. The hole lies near rushes, but has a very good green. The fifth hole is westward and can be carried from the tee shot; it is a nasty hole to get at if not well played from the tee; it is a temper-trying hole but for golf not badly placed. It is clear, from this hole some extension will have to be sought, for reasons that will hereafter appear. The sixth hole is traversed easterly in the direction of the hotel. A good mark is the telegraph post. With a good tee shot, moderately safe ground may be speculated upon but cannot be insured in playing direct for the hole without clearing the rushes altogether, but from this point reached, a short spoon, iron, cleek, or putter (as circumstances indicate) will gain the hole side. Overdone with any of these clubs and the ball will find a rest in the rushes. The seventh hole lies south in a parallel direction with the fourth hole and is in a field which has been furrowed; and, except that it is the same for all, is not golfy near the hole. It takes a drive and a quarter stroke, but is a hole without a putting green, and is capable of being made much better. The eighth hole will show the difference

The "Field" Hole — "not golfy near the hole"

between a good lie and a bad one, and lies in a south-easterly direction. You may get a good lie or a bad one — there is no certainty; and for the second shot there are the post and rails of the racecourse, which you are always hitting or getting behind. You may, however, get pretty close in two good shots and a putter; and the green is decidedly good. The ninth and last hole is due east and may be reached in one good drive, but is not always. When done, it is called a Dun-er or Dunloper. [John Dun was a founder member of Hoylake. *Authors*]. Moderate drivers are content to lie safe and "put" up. The ninth hole is also close to the hotel, and no doubt very good for the proprietor, but query if so good for the player who sometimes, owing to a glass of mild or the reverse, finds his pulse quicker the second half and this is one reason for extending the round; the other reason is that, when in the first year, seventeen couples start, it is clear that in future years the whole round will be blocked up, the first couples coming in before the last have started; and where there is a second half to play, delays and stoppages put golfers off. It may be so, where it must be; but that is no argument for the Hoylake ground, where it need not be; and as there are experienced golfers in the Hoylake Club, they will no doubt explore and find plenty of greens for a more extensive link. On the whole the links are an excellent sample of a very pleasant ground to play on when the wind is not too high, and one which will still improve by playing upon; and where officers are active, the Club prosperous, the lessee an enthusiastic golfer, and the game patronised by the landlord, if Nature is deficient there art will show its handiwork, and the Liverpool Golf Club and golf ground will increase in strength and length.

(from *The Field* November 1869)

Royal Liverpool 1881

Anonymous

No class of golfers, whether north or south of the Tweed, have more reasons to congratulate themselves than those gentlemen who fight under the flag of the "Royal Liverpool". They may well be proud of the history of their club and the glory of its surroundings, for the former is as unique as the latter are in many respects unequalled. Golfers, as a rule, are conservative in their ideas. Unlike the ancient Athenians, who ran after anything that was new, they prefer to hold aloof from aught to which the charm of novelty is attached. Hitherto all first-class golfing societies have been able to boast of lengthy pedigrees and cherished traditions, but the Liverpool Club at one fell blow has shattered all such preconceived notions. Although, comparatively speaking, only a thing of yesterday — having been established in 1869 — it has nevertheless already become a recognised power in the world of golf. To the enthusiasm and energy of those who regulate its destinies this is mainly due, for although the club cannot rank as a venerable body, it is beyond all doubt a vigorous one, and now numbers upwards of five hundred and fifty members on its roll. But to the fame of their head-quarters at Hoylake much of this unprecedented success must be likewise attributed. Liverpudlians have long been loud in praise of their Cheshire golfing arena, which, according, to them, is as near perfection as possible. The late David Strath had, we know, over and over again described it as the best in Britain, and dwelt with fondness on its magnificent natural putting greens. Davie was a shrewd judge — perhaps the least bit inclined to be partial — but there can be no harm in his opinion being corroborated by a Scotch golfer, who has played over every course of note in the kingdom. Hoylake we consider a golfing ground of exceptional excellence, worthy of ranking alongside St. Andrews and Prestwick, partaking in addition, however, very much of the character of the links at Montrose. Bunkers are less plentiful than at the three places named; but deficiency in that respect is amply atoned by the appearance of patches of rank-growing rushes, occasional ditches, and low turf dykes, designated "cops" in the idiom of the district. One marked feature also is the comparative absence of hidden hazards, for, as every golfer knows, it is one of the greatest charms of driving to see the well-hit ball clearing obstacles visible to both player and onlookers. Hoylake surroundings, too, are really grand, and even the most matter-of-fact golfer is a keen student of scenery. The rising ground on which is situated the pretty village of West Kirby, and the wooded hill above, form a fitting adjunct to the green, while the views of the distant West Coast are now and again very beautiful. No society has a more extensive assortment of club plate than has Liverpool, thanks alike to club funds and the liberality of club members. The two principal meetings of the year are the Spring and Autumn ones, and at these visitors from all quarters regularly put in an appearance. Cracks from St. Andrews and Musselburgh, not to mention Blackheath, Westward Ho, and Wimbledon, have ere now appropriated the chief articles of club property, which is perhaps as well, for the new blood, which has recently sprung up, seems quite capable for the future of keeping their own gifts in their own custody.

(from *The Field* December 1881)

The Links in 1896

Guy Farrar

Twenty-five years after the formation of the Club many changes had taken place, and the end of the last century found the links undergoing constant alteration. Two events caused revolutionary changes to be made in the course. The first was the removal of the Club in 1895, from the Royal Hotel to the present Club House, and the second was the lease of the ground on the left of the Long hole, which enabled the present Telegraph and Briars holes to be constructed.

The map shows the layout of the links in the year 1896, when the Club House had just been occupied, but the modern fifth and sixth holes had not yet been made.

The removal to the other side of the links necessitated an alteration in the starting point and the experiment of playing the Royal as the first hole was tried. It proved a failure — players having to cross the present first fairway (then the third) before beginning the round. Obviously this was unsuitable, and the Course finally became the first hole.

The lease of more land enabled the Stanley hole to be abolished as the ground was needed for building purposes, and the Telegraph to be constructed, together with the present Briars hole with its drive over the corner of what was then an orchard.

I have experienced great difficulty in acquiring accurate information about the course of this period. So much change was in progress, that the minds of golfers have become confused, with the passing of years, as to why the alterations occurred. The minutes of the Green Committee record that in places the turf was in very bad condition — the remedy applied being soil and seed. The panacea for all maladies on the greens was rolling, and a suggestion was made that wells should be sunk in different parts of the course, so that water might be obtainable in the summer. The suggestion was carried out, and for many years water for the greens was procured by this method.

The new Clubhouse — note the mower

The following description of the course and the changes which occurred have been written from the somewhat meagre information in the Council and Green Committee minutes, and from the hazy recollection of those who played on the links at that time. To the best of my knowledge the information is correct, but to use a business phrase it is submitted "with errors and omissions excepted."

The holes will be called by names instead of numbers. This will be less confusing as the whole course had to be re-numbered when the new starting point was finally chosen, and again when the Telegraph hole was made. To follow the description reference should be made to the map.

From 1896 onwards THE COURSE (380 yards) was the first hole. Risen out of the old second hole of 1869, it had assumed the shape we know to-day. Beyond the corner of "the Field" on the left of the fairway, a large rabbit warren flourished, extending right up to the green. Hooking at this hole was a costly business in 1896!

THE STANLEY (243 yards) was the second hole. The tee was placed in the middle of a rabbit warren, and the green was on a spot now occupied by some gentleman's dining room. A turf cop — the remains can still be seen on the left of the first fairway — skirted the left edge of the green.

THE ROAD (257 yards), was another short two-shot hole played parallel to Meols Drive. A large isolated bunker probably frightened those who sliced from the tee, and the green (the present second) was guarded by the cross bunker which still protects it. When the Telegraph was made the Stanley disappeared, and the modern Road hole came into being.

THE LONG (468 yards) was played on the same ground used to-day. The tee was much in advance of the present position, and the rushes grew very thickly on the right of the green and on both sides of the fairway, which was intersected by two bunkers — the remnants of which are still to be seen.

THE COP (163 yards) of 1895 would have been quite familiar to our eyes, except that the tee was twenty yards on the right of its present position. The cross bunker was wider in those days, and the "cop" on top of the bunker, from which the hole derived its name, was much higher and consequently the green was less visible.

THE BRIARS (252 yards), before the alteration was made, was a hole played from various tees near the Cop green to the present sixth green. As one can imagine the intervening ground was one mass of briars, rushes, and rough. Two bunkers guarded the entrance, and the famous square shallow hazard — "John Dun's Grave" — was on the left of the green. Major Hopkins has shown this bunker in one of his sketches with its designer caught in his own trap and "wishing that he had not dug it."

THE DOWIE (194 yards), like the Cop would have been quite familiar to us. Three bunkers were in front of the tee, the green being protected by thick rushes without any other hazard.

THE FAR (412 yards) was the same hole as was played up to 1923, the green being in a slight hollow on the left of the present plateau. "Hell" — the bunker to be carried with the second shot — was much larger, and the rough on the left side of the fairway was of a more "tigerish" nature, the home of many lost balls.

THE PUNCH BOWL (328 yards) was in the same position as at present. A bunker was situated at the foot of the sandhill which masks the green, and another hazard — no longer to be seen — appeared in the face of the large sandhill on the right of the fairway. The green was enormous.

THE ALPS (various lengths). The hole was first played (as shown on the map) to a green near the Briars, but later it was moved to the old eleventh green. Played from many different tees on the left of the Punch Bowl, this alteration must have made a trying hole, measuring 538 yards, with a sandhill as a carry for the third

The "Dowie" — sand blow

shot. After a short life it disappeared and the hollow tenth green split this marathon into two holes and restored the Short Alps to life again. At one time the tee was on the left edge of the Punch Bowl green, and drives had to surmount the steep face of a sandhill rising within a few yards of the tee. Special spoons were used to induce the gutty ball to rise over this hazard.

When the elongated Alps was played, it covered the ground now occupied by two holes, making it necessary to introduce another hole to complete the last half of the round.

This difficulty was overcome by constructing the MEOLS hole (170 yards) with a green skirting the hollow on the left of the present sixteenth fairway, and a tee near the Lake green. When the Alps was reduced in length this hole disappeared.

THE SHORT ALPS was originally played as shown on the map. It vanished when the Alps was lengthened, and re-appeared in modern guise when the hollow tenth green was made.

THE HILBRE (300 yards). The tee was near the Short Alps. The green was the same as that played until 1923, with the Pond, and forests of rushes behind.

THE RUSHES (118 yards). The tee shot was played over a waving sea of rushes onto a large green with a cross bunker guarding the entrance. The worst fate that could befall the player was to top a shot, which probably meant a lost ball. Except for the cross bunker, the green was entirely unguarded.

THE FIELD (470 yards). "The hole without a green" of 1869 had vanished,

The "Alps" green

and the present fourteenth, or something like it, had taken its place. Rushes and rabbit holes formed a hazard for the tee shot, and the cross bunker in front of the present fifteenth tee was then in existence — a punishment for a hooked second. The entrance to the green was protected by thick rushes with a bunker defining the right edge.

THE LAKE (402 yards) green is shown on the map as being much to the right of its present position. This I think is a mistake, as, except that the green was then very much nearer the tee, the line of play has hardly altered. A cross bunker stretched in front of the tee, and on the right there was an enormous rabbit warren ready to engulf a slice. Rushes and a single bunker guarded the entrance to the green.

THE DUN (385 yards) was played from a very forward tee to the present green, with the cross bunker a "carry" for the third shot. The line to the hole was round the corner of "the Field" and not across it as shown on the map.

THE ROYAL (344 yards) had a green unprotected by a single hazard, directly opposite the Royal Hotel. The tee was in its present position with the cross-bunker in front.

THE STAND (381 yards). The last green in 1869 was on its present site, protected by a cross bunker with a large colony of rabbit holes on the right of the fairway. In those days more posts — battered and weather-beaten — stretched across the fairway, where now only two remain.

An interesting map drawn by Mr. Leigh Clare in 1897, shows how much the links were changing, because not only has he drawn the holes then played, but also the positions of new greens and tees under consideration. Some of these are in curious places, and it would be interesting to know who made the original suggestions for them. One is shown near the present Hilbre green and another at the end of what is now Stanley Road. A proposed new Dowie green was marked inside the out-of-bounds cop.

When the Telegraph and Briars holes were made, the course again had to be re-numbered, so this period is very difficult to describe, and probably still more difficult to follow when written.

The green staff in "the 'nineties" consisted of Jack Morris and Davis, and between them they had to keep the course in good condition. An extra man was allowed for a few weeks to "get the links in first-class order for the Championship of 1898," as a minute of the Green Committee records. The Council did not always see eye to eye with the Green Committee on the need for expending money on upkeep, and a very tight rein was kept on any extravagance. What their feelings would have been if two thousand pounds had been suggested as a possible annual charge for green expenses, it is difficult to imagine.

During these years much of the original course of 1870 vanished and modern Hoylake began to take shape. Golfers who had not visited the course since 1880 would certainly be unable to find their way round if they played over the links of 1932, but players in 1900 would still discover plenty of holes that could be identified with those planned at this period.

(from *The Royal Liverpool Golf Club* by Guy Farrar, published by Willmer Bros. in 1933)

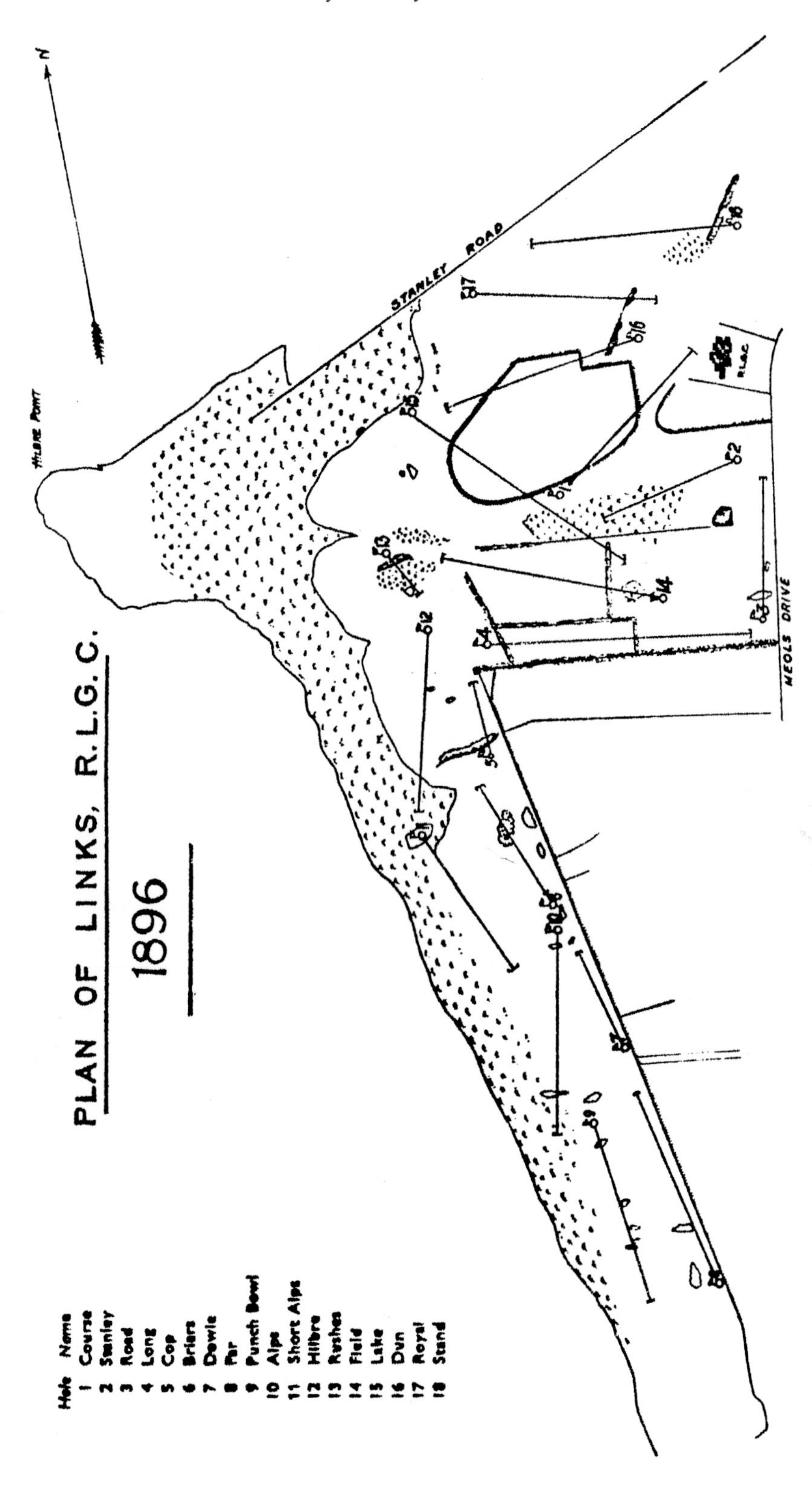
PLAN OF LINKS, R.L.G.C.
1896
Hole Name
1 Course
2 Stanley
3 Road
4 Long
5 Cop
6 Briars
7 Dowie
8 Far
9 Punch Bowl
10 Alps
11 Short Alps
12 Hilbre
13 Rushes
14 Field
15 Lake
16 Dun
17 Royal
18 Stand
HILBRE POINT
STANLEY ROAD
NEOLS DRIVE
R.L.G.C.
N

Changes in the 1920s

Bernard Darwin

What degree of alteration constitutes a reconstructed course? Hoylake for instance has been considerably altered but it has hardly been reconstructed. Yet any material changes on such a course must be named. They are naturally regarded with a jealous eye by lovers of the old, but nobody, I imagine, will deny to Mr. Harry Colt unstinted praise for his eleventh and seventeenth holes, the new Alps and the new Royal. These are changes that count two on the division, for the old holes were poor and the new ones are admirable. The Alps consisted of an entirely blind one-shot hole and had little but its romantic name to recommend it. In its place is another one-shotter from an exhilarating tee to a narrowing green closely beset on one side by the shore and having perfect visibility. But this is a comparatively small improvement compared with that at the Royal. Today with its narrow green between devil of the road on one side and the deep sea of a horrid bunker on the other it is as fine and frightening a seventeenth as anyone can desire, and I imagine that many a reasonably stout heart with a good medal score will be tempted to play it by instalments. It has already been the scene of one classic shot, Walter Hagen's second when he wanted two fours for the Championship. It is worthy to be compared with another seventeenth in which a road plays its part.

The new Hilbre hole

The other three changes, namely the new greens at the Far or eighth hole, and the twelfth or Hilbre and the wholly new thirteenth, which has inherited the old name of the Rushes, are more open to criticism; not on the ground of any lack of ingenuity on the architect's part, but because, fine holes though they are, they are

"Playing to the Briars". This 1893 print depicts John Ball playing a recovery shot, watched by Hilton, Laidlay and Balfour

Harold Hilton in action — oil painting by J.J. Inglis

Aerial view from the north

The Hoylake start and finish from the air (*c.*1962)

The New (4th) green — Brabazon 1989

Early morning — the Telegraph (5th) green

comparatively like many other fine holes to be found elsewhere, whereas those they have superseded were unique; they were essentially Hoylake. This conservatism can be pushed too far; I am ready to give up the old Hilbre, despite the fascination of that open simple approach made frightening by the pond behind the green; but I must shed a tear over the old Far green with its engaging run-in from the right. I cannot quite weep over the old Rushes, but I always remember what John Ball, to be sure an immovable Tory, said about it; that at the old hole the player had to do for himself the work of getting the ball into the air and stopping it on the green, whereas at the new one the high tee did it for him.

I do not criticise the disappearance of the old cross-bunker at the Dun because that had been made inevitable by the modern ball and modern driving. It was sad to see it go if only because the soberest might fall into it after dinner — I have seen them do it — in finding their way home across the darkling links; but it had to go and the present Dun is a fine long hole. Trying not to be Blimpish and die-hard and to look at the course with eyes unblurred by sentiment, I solemnly and sincerely declare that Mr. Colt made a great job of it. When I last watched a Championship there I might sorrow a little that the course and the greens in particular had taken on something of an inlandish perfection and lacked the old hard and ruthless quality that fought ever against the player, but in point of design Hoylake seemed to me as fine a test of the best modern golfers as was to be seen anywhere in the world.

(from the chapter on architecture in *Golf Between Two Wars* published by Chatto & Windus 1944)

Post-War Hoylake

Patric Dickinson

The links of the Royal Liverpool Golf Club is reckoned by everybody to be one of the finest tests of golf in the world. It is depressing to find on seeing it for the first time that it is utterly flat and dreary to look at, and for all the infinite subtleties to be discovered it remains rather formidably unattractive. It is, nowadays, not aesthetically improved by its two fringes of commodious, capacious, but architecturally deplorable villas whence commuters in bowler hats and with brief-cases shuttle to Liverpool.

A visit to Hoylake is rather like one's first visit to the Athenaeum Club. Are these curious and shapeless old gentlemen, bumping and boring round, really the cream of the nation's intellect, carrying each in his own head Wisdom, Knowledge, Infinite Subtlety? Hoylake reminds me inevitably of them; long, slow, inexorable, and *right*. When Professor A. says that there were *No* ninth-century-B.C. spoons; there were, you know, NONE, not a single one — so off the very first tee at Hoylake the first hole dogmatically says: "I am right — you see, you thought you could take liberties with me; no; I am Professor Golf-Par. You missed that four-yarder? but, my dear fellow, there is something faulty in your putting, my greens are perfect." "But...?" "'Perfect,' I said."

The low, artificial two-foot-high banks are a feature of the links; they are called "cops" and run along the edge of fairways. All the holes have names: "the Dun", "the Dowie", etc.; the 4th is called "the Cop". But here there is no cop visible from the usual tees and it is the easiest hole on the course — a typical don's high-table joke. The innumerable out-of-bounds — there are eight — are also like those sharp salty felisities[1] and ripostes on the high table whereby the thrusting Junior Fellows are put in their places. The very making of these cruel, artificial cops on this 'natural' seaside area is typical of Hoylake. Like those compulsory questions in exams — you have got to take notice of them, do them, and then ignore them so that you can get on with what you *do* know. Apart from the cops there is an air of the "wide open spaces" — the area of the links is large, open, bare, agoraphobic: and the wind's paradise, the "haystack and roof-levelling wind".

Hoylake shares with bicycling the strange fact that whichever way you turn, the wind is plumb against, or at any rate unhelpful, across, or only behind when it is downhill, and you don't, anyway (e.g. the 13th), want it to be.

No, once on this Hoylake links, there is no means of avoiding prosecuting counsel's questions. It is a golfing cross-examination which will reveal and work upon every flaw in your golfing technique. It is at Hoylake that all golfing dentists should be forced to take their holidays. Hoylake probes relentlessly, finds the soft spot, and reaches for the drill.

Let us look carefully at the first hole. It is doglegged to the right, round the right angle of two cops: it needs a very long and brave drive to carry the corner. There is plenty of room to the left, and an average stroke will reach the corner, but it is quite easy to go out of bounds. You are left then with a perfectly simple second to the green. But all along the right runs the cop, its mean lowness is an open insult, and along its inside edge is a trough of sand. It is unpardonable but horribly easy to put your second out of bounds, as well as your first.

The second hole takes you towards the villa-tudordom road, and though a certain latitude may be allowed from the tee the approach must be perfect, for the green wears, like a dowager, a collar of precious bunkers: only a high straight pitch-and-stop will do.

There's a cop along the left of the long 3rd and no visible cop at the short 4th called, as we have seen, "The Cop". The fourth tee is right in the middle of the links, and is a good place to survey it from. You are, roughly, facing the line of dunes along the shore and you have the club house at your back. Before you, both left and right, is the most attractive part of the links. The holes from the 5th to the 13th are before you, and these holes constitute the more gentle element of the links. They are, to my mind, the best holes also.

[1] *felis*, a cat.

Now turn inland and face towards the Royal Hotel. There is the famous Hoylake finish; flat, long grinding, and inexorable; to be feared and admired — rather like the finale of Sibelius's Third Symphony: a long, slow winding-up, a steady accumulation and accretion.

If one were to divide Hoylake into the movements of a symphony one would go like this, I think:

1st	Movement	Nos.	1—5
2nd	Movement (andante)		6—12
3rd	Movement (scherzo)		13
4th	Movement		14—18

I would begin my second movement at No. 6, "The Briars", because there one bold stroke from the tee, across a high out-of-bounds corner jutting from the left, takes you into the sea-zone; I would begin it there also because of the slow, steady balance of the holes: 4, 3, 5, 4, 4, 3, 4 they go, though you are not likely to score them perfectly. This is a gentle contemplative passage, not exactly lyrical — as, for instance, the slow movement of Beethoven's Pastoral is not deeply grievous, but a slow, flowing *legato* passage shot through with hints, or with dramatic innuendoes of tragedy. There is the seventh hole, a great short hole, "The Dowie". Another cop crawls sulkily along the left edge of the green, enticing the ball to lip over into outlawry. The green is beautifully modelled and guarded without bunkers, and the ideal shot is a draw just wide enough to turn in and die on to the right-hand side of the green — but a shade too much and out you go.

The 8th undulates up to the far end of the links, and from the ninth tee one sees the whole stretch of the estuary sands and the Welsh coast across the Dee. It is a very pleasant view indeed. Along the sea-dunes in their season bloom thousands of wild briar-roses. They are small plants which make patches of rough along the left, and they give out a wonderfully sweet, pure scent when in flower, and this compounded with a warm western sea-breeze is sheerly magical and restorative to the worn golfer. Of course, if you get among these myriad white eyes your ball becomes a rose, the roses a thousand balls.

Here, farthest away from the asphalt roads of Hoylake, is the place, in June, looking for your ball among the roses, to consider the beliefs of your life and what your monument will be.

Wild flowers on golf links are either weeds or hazards. The roses have a very small practical golfing function and are spared; inland the weed-killers have been at their puritan work in rough as well as fairway. Of course, it is right and proper that they should; but Hoylake is so vast and flat that these austere golfing acres could do with a little innocent decoration. Hoylake is Puritan, yes: a three-hour sermon in a gaunt building, all whitewashed walls and black-clad sinners, or a three-hours round this gloomy, marvellous links, there's not much difference. It's Hell-fire or humble self-surrender to a God who will not tolerate a frivolous stroke, or laughter on the greens. Is golf a game at all, or a form of self-denial, or masochism? Remember that C.E. Jung went one better than Freud and discovered a whole rich vein of sexual symbolism in this game. I am not suggesting that regular players at Hoylake should be psycho-analysed, but I am sure the psycho-analyst should play here also — in combat with the dentist, if possible. I would really like to see a bishop, a dentist, a psycho-analyst, and a professional politician play a series of foursomes round Hoylake. You see, Hoylake is quietly bringing out the venom in me even in meditation upon its most lyrical and pleasant spot: out with it, then, I would like to see them *suffer* ! Let us play the ninth hole, which is easy and old-fashioned, into a punch-bowl of a green. The 10th, 11th, and 12th are beautiful, excellent golf holes.

And the short, wicked 13th, cocking a snook inland like "a little vulgar boy", at the whole cold grind to come, is exactly like the *scherzo* of a symphony: gay, jiggety, tricky, witty, deplorable perhaps, but what a relief!

Then the finale begins. The 14th is called the "Field", rightly, and is a gruelling flat slog along: the 15th brings you back again almost parallel. Both these holes are open and free.

The 16th is doglegged to the right over the cop-made corner of the rectangular practice field, and more 5's are taken here than 4's, even in bounds. The "Royal" goes towards the Royal Hotel, just across the road from the green, which lies at an awkward angle to the road, like a mat just askew from the hearth. You can get to the green in 2, or be in the road in 2, or play short. The Royal Hotel, a late-eighteenth-century barracky building — but the one piece of genuine architecture for miles — was built for the bathing craze of the period, fell into desuetude and revived as a golfers' hotel in the seventies. It was then owned by the great John Ball's grandfather.

The 18th, like the 2nd, has a necklace of bunkers. It is called the "Stand", for this is where the Liverpool Hunt Club had their racecourse, and it is on this inland half of the links that golf was begun in 1869.

Hoylake is a tough, epic links. Like one of those classics of literature which one is always being recommended to read — "You won't really enjoy it, but you *must* read it, it is an experience you will never forget ... and it is beautifully written."

You cannot just walk into Hoylake any more than you can walk into the Athenaeum and ask for a half of bitter. You must be introduced by a real live member: in person, or by letter. Decorum must be observed. Club servants in livery pad about silently and look melancholy, as good club servants always must, in order that the members may feel the happier for seeing them.

When you have played you will be asked, "What do you think of the greens?" You will notice a sudden tension in the air. Hoylake has been waiting since 1869 for somebody to say "...", but you will say, "Wonderful". Everybody will relax — and you may go, now.

(from *A Round of Golf Courses* published by Evans Brothers Ltd 1951)

Bunkered at the new 3rd Hole

An Exercise in Fear

Pat Ward Thomas

Hoylake is unique among British championship links because it is possible to be out-of-bounds within the confines of the course, and innumerable golfers have condemned it on this count. Until 1920 the penalty for out-of-bounds was loss of distance only and thus the golfers of old were not so harshly punished. Now, Hoylake can inflict the tortures of the damned. There is always an alternative to flirting with danger, but what an exercise in fear some of those holes can be.

The right angle of the 1st makes a forbidding opening hole. On the left from the tee is the clubhouse with its silken putting green; on the right, for the full length of the hole, is the sinister "cop", a bank no more than three feet high which encloses the practice ground. A good drive will finish past the corner, but a long shot remains with the haunting thought that a slice will be fatal if one aims for the green, which is hard against the cop. Many a player has been out-of-bounds with his drive and approach; many have run out of hope or ammunition before completing the hole. It is a fiendish 19th.

Before the 3rd was changed, and a fine new short 4th created in readiness for the 1967 Open, the slightest pull would sail out-of-bounds over another cop. But now the golfer is free until the 6th. This is the famous Briars, where a high-fenced orchard is in line for the drive; against a strong prevailing wind the carry from the back tee is terrible to behold.

No hole in Britain has caused more argument than the 7th, named Dowie after Hoylake's founder. The narrow ellipse of green is protected on the left by yet another cop, and it is possible to hit a perfect long iron to the heart of the green and see the ball hop over the bank out-of-bounds within a few yards of the flag. Unless the green is soft, to aim at the flag is either heroic or stupid depending on the state of the game. To play safely out to the right leaves a tricky chip through a little swale. In the last round of the Open in 1930 Jones needed two fours to be out in 35. After two long shots over the crumpled 8th fairway he was no more than fifteen yards from the green but, as he wrote later, he took seven for the hole "in the most reasonable manner possible". His torment of mind is only too easy to imagine; so too is the enormous effort of will and control that enabled him to finish just safe from pursuit. This was the second leg of the "quadrilateral".

From the 8th the golf is of the old, true seaside character, dipping and curving along the sandhills, with estuary at hand, silver and grey, or golden when the tide is down; Hilbre Island and its myriad birds and the quiet hills of Wales are in the distance. The 9th with its bowl of a green, the superb short 11th, and the Alps, its green an oblong oasis in the dunes, the lovely sweep of the 12th, and the tightest of pitches to the 13th with its necklace of bunkers, make a splendid prelude to the long, long finish on the plain below.

Now the field comes into play again. It is possible to slice into it from the 15th tee, and its corner cuts clean across the direct line to the 16th, 533 yards long. This hole was decisive in the last round of the 1967 Open when Jack Nicklaus and the sentimental favourite Roberto de Vicenzo fought a superbly entertaining duel. Nicklaus, playing ahead, scored a birdie-four, before Vicenzo struck his drive to the very edge of the field. From there he hit a soaring spoon to make sure of a birdie and the title.

Of all the finishing holes at Hoylake the 17th can make the greatest play on courage and fear. A cool, firm contrary wind emphasizes the severely taxing nature of the hole where the green is angled across the line of flight, with a road flanking its far side and approaches. The slightest overhit, cut or pushed second shot can easily trickle out-of-bounds under the fence, while the cautious, playing to the left, risk deep bunkers from where the recovery must be played towards the road, a disagreeable prospect. To have a reasonable shot for the flag the drive must hold the right side of the fairway and escape the bunkers that lurk there for the shot that leaks, as shots are inclined to leak in times of stress. Although the last hole is not overly demanding, the man who has played the last five in fours is no mean golfer.

(from *The World Atlas of Golf* published by Mitchell Beazley 1976)

The Hoylake Open Championships

1897 Open — Harold Hilton

Harold H. Hilton

Editor's note : At the end of the first day Hilton, with a 36 hole total of 155 was a stroke behind Braid, and 3 ahead of Tait, but an 84 in the third round sent him in to lunch "a very sick and peevish man", as Braid now had 3 strokes in hand. He had also been overtaken by Tait, Pulford and Herd, who were all a shot ahead of him.

I cannot say that this affected my lunch, as on top of many good things I finished up with some trifle, simply on the recommendation of an individual not unassociated with the inner management of the Royal Liverpool Club, who confidently asserted that it was the finest thing in the world on which to do a 75 — as events turned out, one of the truest things he has said in this world.

When I arrived on the tee my old friend Paxton greeted me with the remark, "Now, Mr. Hilton, a 75 this afternoon, nothing more." The number 75 seemed to be in the air. The start was very auspicious, as a putt of fifteen to twenty yards found the bottom, and a three was placed on the card; a four came at the second, and then there came a shot which might have ended in serious disaster. In the three previous rounds the wind had been nearly dead behind the players, and it had been necessary to play very carefully to remain short of the bunker. I had noticed, however, that the wind had been gradually changing, and instead of being behind, was inclined to be across. First I addressed the ball with my spoon, and then changed my mind and took a longer club to get as near the bunker as possible. Just as I was addressing the ball my caddie, who was becoming a little excited, remarked, "Take care; you will get in with that." I simply remarked, "Will you shut up?" — not very courteous certainly, but I did know the Hoylake links. The result of the shot was disastrous, as I cut across it, and it pitched right into a little bunker beside the "Field" green. I saw the sand fly up. When I arrived on the scene I found fortune on my side, as the ball had pitched in the bunker, and in so doing had thrown up a little mound of sand on which the ball was perched, the only difficulty being that there was a bank in front of me. I decided, however, to go for it, and taking my spoon I played for a hook, brought the shot off and holed out in five. A very useful two followed at the next hole, and a four was quite satisfactory at the fifth hole. A total of 18 for the first five holes was more than satisfactory, and I had no ambition to play them ever again. When, however, one starts in this sensational fashion, and then has a little time to deliberate upon the question of possibilities, as one invariably has in a big field in the Open Championship, thoughts and fancies pass through the mind, and these thoughts and fancies are apt to upset the equilibrium of the most staid of players. Whether this happened in my case or not I cannot say, but there is one thing certain and that is that for a short spell I tried my best to discount this great start, and began to play the fool on the green at the very next hole. As my second shot left me but a few yards from the pin, I promptly putted short, and followed this up by missing a very short one. The seventh or "Dowie" hole is always a trying one, and it has always been a hole which I have had reason to remember as an enemy, nor on this occasion did it prove any exception to the rule. In the three previous rounds I had played it a little too safely, and on each occasion had taken four to it. On the present occasion I determined to play boldly for the green, with the result that I held the ball too much into the wind and it just pitched out of bounds. Number two was more successful, as it finished close to the hole; but once again three putts were required, and I began to realise that I was gradually dissipating a glorious chance. A five to the eighth was quite satisfactory, but another stroke went astray at the ninth, as once again three strokes were required on the green; I found myself therefore with a total of 38 for the outward journey, and at one time I had had dreams and visions of 36 or something under that figure. And, what was worse, the harder part of the journey had to be overcome, for a great deal of this journey had to be played against a head-wind.

Whilst standing on the tee to the tenth, I heard that Freddie Tait was also out in 38, which was not at all comforting news, as it meant that he still held a lead of one stroke. I always consider that the first four holes home on the Hoylake course are exceedingly crucial ones in a medal round. They comprise that portion of the course where it is either possible for a man to pull himself together and transform an average beginning into quite a respectable score, or back up a good outward journey in such a fashion that except for extreme disaster in the last five holes, a good total is ensured. Now, fortunately for me, I got those holes in schedule numbers, viz., four, three, four, three. In doing so I had one piece of good fortune, in that at the eleventh, or "Alps" hole, I laid a short pitch from the top of the hill literally stone dead. This little help brought my score down to an average of fours. The "Field" hole was a trying one that day and I was very thankful to leave it in the rear with an orthodox five. Then came a little bit of fortune which was extremely useful, as at the "Lake" hole I ran down a very useful putt for a four, and I knew well that at this stage every stroke must make a difference. This gave me heart of grace, and I played the "Dun" hole confidently, and this notwithstanding that I had to wait a very long time before I could play my second shot; but I had my nerves well in control, and was determined not to be bustled, and I did not strike until the course in front was absolutely clear of spectators. Down in five I was left with a four and a five for 75; but the five came first, as I was terribly short both with my approach and my approach putt to the seventeenth, and missed my fourth.

Now in the three previous rounds it was literally an impossibility for me to reach the last green in two, but I had noticed during the round that the wind had been gradually whipping round from the east to the north, and in place of being almost dead ahead at this hole, it was now almost directly across the line of the hole; in consequence I decided to have a go at my tee shot in the hope that I might get over in two. I had a go, and got fairly hold of the ball, but when I came up to it I found that, notwithstanding that I had really hit the shot, there were still grave doubts as to whether I could get home. My caddie handed me a club with which to play short, but I had a good look at it, and decided to have a dash at it. I had plenty of time in which to weigh up the pros and cons of the situation, for the couple in front seemed to be playing some kind of game of their own on the green; they may, in fact, have been not at all slow, but to me it seemed an interminable time. I badly wanted to get this shot over, as the more I looked at it the less I liked it. At last came the welcome signal, and without wasting any time over preliminaries I let go. The ball went as true as steel off the club, but unfortunately I had the slightest bit of pull on the stroke, and I knew well that the farther you go to the left at this hole the longer is the carry.

Harold Hilton

Directly they saw the ball sail away from the club, the spectators began to cheer and clap; they promptly took it for granted that it must clear the bunker, but I knew that it was a case of touch and go. I had played that hole far too often, and in my anxiety I mentally stigmatised them as fools for their somewhat premature applause. I should not have been at all surprised had the ball plumped straight into the bunker, but it got over, by how much I cannot say; I have an idea that it must have been more a question of feet than yards, as by the way it jumped it must have landed on the bank just over the hazard; but "all's well that ends well," and it was over and close to the hole. Putt number one was not at all a bold one. One spectator called it a drunken effort, and he was not far wrong. Putt number two dobbled about, and eventually made its entry into the hole at the back door, but it got there, and that was everything. I can see that ball now hesitating on the lip of the hole like a helpless derelict.

Editor's note : As an early starter Hilton had to wait an hour or so before Braid his chief rival came into view. Tait had already missed his chance by dropping shots on the inward holes.

... I didn't make any inquiries as to details, however, but to relieve my feelings went into the billiard-room and tried to play a game with a kindly friend, who sacrificed himself on my behalf. I cannot think that I took much interest in that game, for I was soon at the club window watching the enemy playing the sixteenth hole, and I cannot say I was sorry to see him take six for the hole. Looking from the window I could not make much of the proceedings to the seventeenth, but the hole took so long to play that I came to the conclusion that the total was more likely to be five than four, and I summoned up enough pluck to wander out again to see the finish, and the first thing I heard was a shout, "He's a three to tie." I felt quite a brave man again, as I knew that last hole at Hoylake. It is always a good four, and an exceptional three, and, moreover, on this occasion there were one or two reasons which made it all the more difficult. Firstly, the wind was if anything against the player; not that this would stop Braid from getting home in two, but it necessitated a long approach in place of a short one. Again the hole was placed in a most difficult position. Mr. Ryder Richardson told me that he had never seen such terrible putting in his life as he had at this hole. Nearly every one had been skating about round the hole like small children, and he had hardly seen a decent putt holed during the whole of the two days' play.

In my own mind I could not see Braid or any one else doing that hole in three, and I felt that the championship was in my pocket. I had an anxious moment or two, however. To begin with, his drive was one of the best, and it was very evident that he could easily get home in two. First he took out a wooden club, then hesitated and walked some distance forward, and eventually decided to take an iron one. In James Braid's long career he has probably seldom played a finer stroke than that second of his to this last hole in 1897; it was never off the pin. Everything depended upon the roll of the ball. On it came, and nobody could accurately tell where it would stop. Fortunately for me the green was keen, and it kept trickling along, passed within a foot or so of the hole, and did not stop until it had rolled some six or eight yards past. As befitted the occasion, he took any amount of pains over that putt; but, personally, I felt very confident as to the result. I knew that hole and its position, and, moreover, the putt was a difficult one. He made an excellent bid, but the ball skidded past on the left-hand side, and I once again said, "Thank heaven."

(from *My Golfing Reminiscences* published by Nisbet & Co. 1907)

LEADING SCORES

Mr. H.H. Hilton	80	75	84	75	=	314
J. Braid	80	74	82	79	=	315
Mr. F.G. Tait	79	79	80	79	=	317
G. Pulford	80	79	79	79	=	317
A. Herd	78	81	79	80	=	318
H. Vardon	84	80	80	76	=	320
A. Simpson	83	81	81	79	=	324
D. Brown	79	82	80	83	=	324
T. Vardon	81	81	79	83	=	324
J.H. Taylor	82	80	82	86	=	330
A. Kirkaldy	83	83	82	82	=	330
Mr. S. Mure Fergusson	87	83	79	82	=	331
Ben Sayers	84	78	85	84	=	331

1902 Open — Sandy Herd

Sandy Herd

I arrived at Hoylake two days before the championship began, and well remember taking out of my bag a grand new Shetland golfing coat, a present from Mr. Crowther, who said as he gave it to me, "Sandy, this is for luck; you can give it back to me when you're done with it, as a souvenir." I wore that coat all through the championship and it was greatly admired.

I started practice straight away and found my form immediately. One of the first gentlemen I met was Mr. John Ball, in my opinion the greatest amateur golfer that ever swung a club. Although he is now nearly sixty years of age, I should not put it past him to add a ninth to the eight amateur championships he has already won. We arranged to play my first practice round together, and from that moment Mr. Ball took as much interest in me as if we had been lifelong friends.

He was using the Haskell ball, and doing such wonders with it that I found myself envying him. I had not seen the rubber-cored ball before, and when we reached the fifteenth hole, Mr. Ball, smiling at my comments regarding his drives, gave me a Haskell to try.

That was the end of the gutta ball for me. The first drive I made with the Haskell was longer than any drive I had ever made with the gutta, and what impressed me chiefly was that the Haskell could be driven without any effort.

On returning to the Club House I made straight for Jack Morris's shop to secure some Haskells. Jack was a very reverend-looking gentleman, like his uncle, old Tom Morris, of St. Andrews. He was only able to give me four Haskells, but my joy was unbounded.

I did a 77, which was neither very good nor very bad, only fair, and, all things considered, a poorer performance than I ought to have made. Harry Vardon started off with the wonderful score of 72, but in the afternoon he took 77, making the wonderful total of 149 for the two rounds. The general opinion was that Vardon would win again, for the fourth time. I knocked up a very nice 76, giving me a total of 153, which satisfied me that I could do better. Ted Ray tied with me for second place, and James Braid was third with 154. My old friend, Andrew Kirkaldy, tied with Mr. Hilton at 155, only two shots behind myself, six shots behind Vardon.

The second day was the decisive one, which ended in the happiest way for me. Not in all my golfing career can I think of a red-letter day like that, when all my young dreams came true; for did I not as a boy frequently go as early as four in the morning to the first hole at St. Andrews and say to myself as I practised putting, "You have this to win the championship"?

I had the good fortune to be drawn with Mr. John Ball for the third round, and I do not hesitate to say, at this distance of years, that Mr. Ball was much more desirous that I should win than that he should beat me. He played his best, to be sure, but in many quiet ways — all within the rules, of course — he gave me every encouragement that one man could give another. In fact, I often wonder whether I owed my victory more to John Ball than to the Haskell ball — poor joke, but let it go. I played like one inspired against a very troublesome wind and returned a score of 73.

Sandy Herd

Some idea of the quality of my golf at this round may be gathered from the fact that Harry Vardon and James Braid both took eighty strokes, so that at the end of the third round I led by three strokes from Vardon and eight from Braid. Could I hold on to my advantage?

All the bogeys of the past, when championships have slipped through my fingers, seemed to troop alongside of me in the last round, and I finished with a score of 81 — distinctly below my form.

You can picture me waiting for Vardon on the last green, with Mr. Ball standing beside me, fully understanding my thoughts. When I learned that Harry had a six-foot putt to tie with me, my feelings can be imagined. I saw him take a good look at the putt, going down on his right knee to see the line. In those days Harry Vardon rarely missed putts of that distance with the gutta. Fortunately for me, this was one of the rare occasions. I should not have cared to be photographed as I watched that putt of his come up straight for the hole and then stop on the lip. I did not say "Hard luck," being too grateful for my own good luck. So that was Harry out of the way.

My hopes were beginning to rise until James Braid came along to give me a second fright. Though I led him by eight strokes for the last round, he came hot after me. Requiring a 73 to tie, he just failed with a wonderful round of 74. I watched him very nearly hole a long putt to equal my score. I breathed again and knew now that the goal of my ambition was reached, for I feared none else but Vardon and Braid.

(from *My Golfing Life* published by Chapman & Hall 1923)

LEADING SCORES

A. Herd	77	76	73	81	=	307
H. Vardon	72	77	80	79	=	308
J. Braid	78	76	80	74	=	308
Mr. R. Maxwell	79	77	79	74	=	309
T. Vardon	80	76	78	79	=	313
J.H. Taylor	81	76	77	80	=	314
J. Kinnell	78	80	79	77	=	314
Mr. H.H. Hilton	79	76	81	78	=	314
E. Ray	79	74	85	80	=	318
A. Kirkaldy	77	78	83	82	=	320
A. Massy	77	81	78	84	=	320

1907 Open — Arnaud Massy

John Graham

The Championship format had changed. Half the field played two qualifying rounds on the Tuesday and the other half on the Wednesday. The successful contestants qualified for the Championship proper, playing two rounds on the Thursday and two on the Friday.

The first qualifying day was a very wet one. It poured torrents all day. Arnaud Massy, of La Boulie near Versailles in France, led this group with a remarkable score of 73 + 74 = 147. He was five strokes ahead of Alex Herd on 152.

The weather on the second qualifying day was even worse. Although the rain had ceased, it blew a gale all day. In the second rounds, during the afternoon, only three players beat 80. J.H. Taylor had the best qualifying score with 76 + 78 = 154.

The Championship proper started the next day. The weather was just as bad with a gale from the south west, and rain in the afternoon. In the morning only four players beat 80. The most difficult hole seems to have been the 6th (The Briars). Of the 67 would-be champions, nine players took 8s (including James Braid and Tom Vardon) and eleven took 7s (including Harry Vardon). Only two players scored 4s. In the afternoon John Ball actually took 9 at this hole.

Another hole that caused some discomfort was The Cop (4th hole), so called because of a raised bank behind a ditch a yard or two from the tee. On that Thursday morning the tee was placed perilously close to the Cop with the result that sixteen players actually hit it (including James Braid) with varying degrees of misadventure. That hole has now gone, but the more elderly members will remember it well.

"Massy's tee shot at the Cop"

After the first two rounds Arnaud Massy led the field with two fine rounds of 76 + 81 = 157, one stroke ahead of J.H. Taylor of Richmond and Tom Ball of West Lancashire. At this stage it seemed a distinct possibility that a foreigner might win the Open Championship for the first time. The Frenchman was playing well. His driving was immaculate and his putting steady, though not brilliant.

The last day of the Championship drew good crowds. The weather had improved somewhat. It was expected that J.H. Taylor would outlast the Frenchman because of his superior experience. But Taylor knew that he was up against a doughty opponent. After the first day's qualifying rounds, it was Taylor himself who remarked "Arnaud Massy would just about win the Championship". At the end of the third round Taylor had drawn one ahead of Massy who had not unexpectedly had a poor start.

The decisive moments really came at the first three holes of the final round with Taylor scoring 5, 4, 7 against Massy's 5, 3, 5. Taylor ruined his chances when he sliced his second shot at the third hole into really deep rough and took two shots to reach the fairway. He finished his round with a score of 80, and Massy, with a final round of 77, won the Championship by two strokes.

The Frenchman finished his round at about six o'clock in the evening in front of an estimated 4,000 spectators. Although the Cup was destined for foreign parts, he was given a hearty cheer and his brother professionals rushed forward and shouldered him halfway to the Clubhouse. He was a very popular winner.

Two comments, perhaps, might be made. Firstly it was probably the worst weather ever encountered in an Open Championship. J.H. Taylor in an article in *Golf Illustrated* shortly afterwards, wrote:

> The Open Championship of 1907 will be known in the years that are to come as Massy's Championship. It will be more indelibly fixed in the minds and memories of those who competed in it as the Championship of continuous hurricane winds interspersed with torrential rains. I have competed annually for the past fifteen years, and I do not remember a Championship contested in anything like such weather. It blew very hard on the first day at Sandwich in 1894, but it was a zephyr breeze compared to the hurricane that raged at Hoylake. Hoylake, even under normal conditions, is a terribly difficult course to play; under the conditions that existed a fortnight ago it was simply fearful. Speaking personally, I can safely say that never have I played golf under such heartbreaking and nerve-racking conditions. There was not a single stroke that one was called upon to play during the round that could be termed easy. You were fighting the wind the whole of the time and with every shot, the odds being greatly against the player. It was not a wind that blew steadily hard from one point of the compass. On the contrary, it continually changed its quarter in a most bewildering manner and with great rapidity, thereby increasing tenfold the difficulties of the position. It prevented one from being accustomed to any particular stroke, and kept the player "on the stretch" the whole of the time. If a stroke had to be played down the wind, one's whole mind and energies were concentrated in trying to stop the ball somewhere near the hole. One could not afford to play at the hole, and this was most apparent with the second shots at the second, twelfth, fourteenth, sixteenth and eighteenth holes. It was also a fact that the most naturally difficult holes were made infinitely more so owing to these adverse conditions.

Secondly, George Pulford, a freelance professional from Hoylake, finished joint third. He was a much better golfer than generally thought. He had finished fourth in the 1895 Open and joint third in 1897. On the Saturday before the 1907 Championship, the English Professionals played the Scottish Professionals over 36 holes at Hoylake. George Pulford, playing for England, defeated the famous Willie Park by 9 and 8. So there was some form behind him. Furthermore, John Graham, of the Royal Liverpool, was the leading Amateur with John Ball one stroke behind him. The local golfers did not do too badly!

Arnaud Massy was a Basque from Biarritz. He was tall, muscular and very erect with strong shoulders and a heavy moustache. In his early days he was a sardine fisher but spent his spare time playing pelota and also caddying for English visitors to the resort. From watching them he developed a free and graceful style. He was first of all left handed, but discarded that when he decided to take the game seriously. He modelled his early golf largely on Horace Hutchinson. Just before the end of the century, he was brought to Britain to complete his golfing education. North Berwick became his headquarters and, under the watchful eye of Ben Sayers, he matured into a fine prospect. When he arrived in Scotland he was a hot-headed Frenchman, but that national disadvantage he managed to overcome. His rounds at Hoylake were calmness personified, especially during the last one. He had an open stance and played his shots with no fuss. His grip was two-handed with the left thumb stuck into the palm of his right hand and down the shaft (no Vardon grip for him). He was a long hitter of the ball and a fine cleek player. During the Championship his wife (he married a Miss Henderson from North Berwick) gave birth to a daughter. He was so delighted at winning the Open that he called her "Hoylake".

1907 Champion

Massy's win was a salutory shock to the British golf world. No longer could important British Championships be regarded as the prerogative of the British. The Amateur Championship of 1904 had been won by W.J. Travis, an American, and now the Open had gone to a Frenchman. The foreign invasion of British supremacy at golf had begun. France was naturally delighted at the result. At last national revenge had been gained on the old enemy as the following ode which appeared in *Golf Illustrated* at the time, made amply clear.

Arnaud le Conquerant

Je me souviens
Des jours anciens
Crécy, Poitiers, Trafalgar, Waterloo,
Et je pleure.
Mais je mange le Bifteck,
Et je pense de Hoylake,
Et je ris.
C'est la Revanche,
J'ai traversé La Manche,
Personne ne m'empéche.
Paisablement j'ai joué
Angleterre j'ai conquis;
Voilà tout!

LEADING SCORES

Arnaud Massy	76	81	78	77	=	312
J.H. Taylor	79	79	76	80	=	314
G. Pulford	81	78	80	76	=	317
Tom Vardon	81	81	80	75	=	317
E. Ray	83	80	79	76	=	318
James Braid	82	85	75	76	=	318
G. Duncan	83	78	81	77	=	319
T. Williamson	82	77	82	78	=	319
Harry Vardon	84	81	74	80	=	319
Tom Ball	80	78	81	81	=	320
P.J. Gaudin	83	84	80	76	=	323
A. Herd	83	81	83	77	=	324
Mr. John Graham	83	81	80	82	=	326
W. Toogood	76	86	82	82	=	326

1913 Open — J.H. Taylor

J.H. Taylor

Of the five British Championships I have won, my win at Hoylake in 1913 ranks second in my regard as a proud accomplishment. My first at Sandwich in 1894 stands alone. My attempts to win on the Cheshire links in 1897 and 1902 had not been conspicuously successful and my being beaten into second place by Massy in 1907 had engrained the belief that Hoylake was not to my liking or one that suited my style of play. This was disappointing, as ever since my caddie days at Westward Ho I had looked upon Hoylake as a second home — in those early days it was the next-door neighbour — the home of my other golfing hero, Johnnie Ball; and the thought that perhaps for ever I should be thwarted from winning there not only disturbed my equanimity, but also injured my pride. I began to realize that if 1913 should prove to be abortive, my chances were as a closed book. It was now or never. Earlier in this chapter I have told that in trying to relate my championship attempts since 1907 I have had to rely on my not-too-trustworthy memory, owing to lack of any accurate data, and when my persuasive and kind friend, Mr. Bernard Darwin, intimated to me, when he knew I was trying to write this book, that he hoped I would let myself go — or words to that effect — on the subject of the 1913 Championship, I had to set about getting some authentic details of it in order that memory should not take a leading and perhaps misleading part in its recital.

A good friend, for over thirty years, came to my assistance in the person of Mr. D.M. Mathieson, the editor and publisher of *Golf Monthly*, and kindly lent me copies of that journal to enable me to get the scores correct, which, after all, is what mostly matters. Before the Championship proper began I received one of the biggest frights of my life. I qualified to take part in it without a single stroke to spare. Most of the competitors had finished the qualifying two rounds as I was playing the thirty-sixth hole and I remember inquiring most anxiously from George Duncan what the qualifying total was and it came as a shock, after a rapid arithmetical calculation, that a five was necessary to enable me to get in. The last hole at Hoylake is not a difficult four, a driver and a pitch over the cross bunker on to the green. Most probably it was nerves, but whatever happened I failed to get properly hold of the ball with my pitch shot and into the bunker it went. I dug it out into some rough stuff at the back, scuffled it out to within a couple of yards of the hole and all my hopes were now centred on my holing the putt. As I faced up to it I remember saying to myself: "Well, Taylor my lad, there's only one place for this and that's the bottom of the hole." I can see that putt now. It was none too easy as the intervening ground was shiny and slippery from much treading and it appeared horribly bare. But the devilish thought uppermost in my mind was the knowledge that if I missed I should need to pack up and go home. The grisly alternative may have acted as an incentive and the word relief is not sufficiently intense in its meaning to describe how I felt when I saw the ball disappear, dropping in with a sickening wobble on the right-hand side, a sure indication that the ball was not struck with firmness and conviction. I have always maintained that the qualifying round is a more exacting test than the Championship proper. In the latter one may play a first round of mediocre quality knowing that three remain in which the defect may be remedied, but a poor first round in the qualifying stage means the end, and that, believe me, is not a comforting or inspiring reflection when on the first tee.

After twenty-eight years I shall be forgiven for not remembering the brand of weather that existed on the first day of the Championship, but that it was favourable the scores of those who led the field is a reliable indication. As befitted the reigning champion Ray headed the list with 147, I followed with 148, Michael Moran 150, Vardon 154 and Johnnie McDermott, the American, making his second and last attempt to win, 155. Mike Moran, a small wiry type of Irishman, was a fine player and like most of his race a rare tryer and typically enthusiastic. To find myself so comfortably placed in the rear of Ted, with Vardon six strokes behind and Braid a long way down the list gave me the feeling that perhaps my Hoylake luck was about to change and I went to bed in a hopeful frame of mind.

The pleasant nature of the weather that ended the day's exertion showed no sign of any alteration on retiring, but during the night a gale of wind sprang up with a suddenness that I was told is not unusual on that part of the coast. I know something of what a gale of wind is like, but this visitation was much worse that I ever experienced. It was a full-throated hurricane, the wind blowing in intermittent gusts that were overwhelming, and it was accompanied with sheets of torrential rain, a dismal and depressing prospect as I went downstairs for an early breakfast. I was timed to start at nine twenty-five, and the sight of the large marquees and smaller tents (erections which give to the scene the sense of commercial activity and usefulness at championship time and is, by the way, a modern innovation) flattened to the ground by the wind as I made my way to the club house was depressing enough to crush every optimistic desire and outlook. As I passed the first tee — dear old Jack Morris on faithful duty like the Roman sentry of historical interest — I stopped to watch Moran drive off and play around the corner. Mike was a light-weight, and it is but the exact truth to state that he found it almost impossible to stand up to the ball and swing the club. I saw him play five shots before rounding the bend and a few minutes later word came that he had taken ten for the hole and his chance virtually gone. I was sorry for Mike then, but was sorrier still when we heard some eighteen months later that he had been killed in the war when fighting as a trooper in the Irish Horse.

Let me give the reason why Braid was so far down the list. His eyesight was never strong and about this time it was giving him and all his friends much anxiety. As a restful measure he was advised to give up playing for a time and was strongly dissuaded from playing in the Championship, a sacrifice he was unwilling to make, so it was a strange and pathetic sight to see him wearing darkly tinted glasses, battling along with vision restricted but with magnificent courage. (He had won his five British Championships, as I have said, in the space of nine years — a feat that will be remembered for all time.) It was a serious cause for anxiety among his multitude of friends, but one which happily was soon removed. ... I wish I had been endowed with an imagination and the gift of words to enable me to write in language that would arrest my reader's attention to the point of wonder, but as I cannot claim such power, I can only hope that what I have to say about my playing this particular round will, as it must, satisfy. I shall not be blamed for confessing that I don't remember any outstanding incident. I do remember, however, that after being sent off on my journey by Jack Morris, who wished me luck, it took me two full wooden club shots to get opposite the corner — fortunately the wind was blowing off the out of bounds copse, so that I could afford to hug it closely — and another full brassie shot failed to reach the green, but I got a creditable five by laying my long 'run-up' dead. Down the wind at the second the difficulty was to hold the pitch back and prevent the ball racing far beyond the hole, and another five was the best I could do. The long dreary third was slap into the eye of the gale and from the tee the green looked to be an immeasurably long distance away. It took me three full clouts and I then found myself sixty yards short, but laying a low running iron shot to within a couple of yards and holing the putt I again got what must have been the best five I ever

J. H. Taylor driving at the 10th

obtained. All this time, and it continued, the rain was coming down in drenching sheets, and I was accompanied by a few faithful followers. One gentleman conferred on me an eternal obligation and I wish I could remember his name. I suspected he had backed me to win, but it was no suspicion but an actual fact that he must have raided the lavatories and annexed half a dozen towels which he carried under his waterproof and which he withdrew one by one to enable me to dry my hands between each stroke.

The sixth or Briars hole at Hoylake is rightly judged to be one of the most difficult in the world of golf. With a bit of wind against, as is usual, it presents a real problem and many a thousand players have come to utter grief when playing it. The slightest draw on the tee shot and away the ball goes out of bounds into the garden; and those many others who deem caution the better part of valour, try to steer the shot between its corner on the left and the clumps of furze bushes on the right, are perhaps the more commendable (remember I am writing of twenty-eight years ago, a gale of wind blowing and when the tee was far back.) When I faced it that morning it appeared an almost impossible proposition. I got my five by risking the bushes from the tee, playing a safe second and a pitch and a couple of putts gave it me. I should like to give my figures for the outward and remainder of the long tiring homeward journey. I had framed the four identical score cards of these two days' blood and sweat, so that I can vouch for the accuracy of these figures:

Out	5 4 5 4 4 5 3 5 5 —	40
In	4 4 4 3 5 5 5 4 3 —	37
		77

I then considered, as I still do, that it was the finest round I ever played. Ray finished in 81, Vardon 79 and Mike Moran 89 which gave me a lead of three strokes.

The wind died down a little and the rain stopped during the afternoon's play. The only incident I remember worth recalling is that I got the Briars in three, taking a bolder course than in the morning, carrying the corner of the garden and ripping home a driving mashie shot which nearly knocked the pin out and left the ball a foot or so beyond the hole. I don't remember whether Mr. Darwin saw the stroke, Mr. Croome certainly did, and his description of it, that "the ball seemed to make a hole in the wind as it bored its way along" is one of which I have always been intensely proud. I finished the final round in 79, Ray taking 84 and Vardon 80, so the satisfaction was given me of achieving my ambition of winning a championship at Hoylake and that with eight shots to spare.

(from *Golf: My Life's Work* published by Jonathan Cape 1943)

The "Royal" green — Vardon putting

LEADING SCORES

J.H. Taylor	73	75	77	79	=	304
E. Ray	73	74	81	84	=	312
M. Moran	76	74	89	74	=	313
H. Vardon	79	75	79	80	=	313
T.G. Renouf	75	78	84	78	=	315
J.J. McDermott	75	80	77	83	=	315
J. Sherlock	77	86	79	75	=	317
J. Bradbeer	78	79	81	79	=	317
A. Massy	77	80	81	79	=	317
T. Williamson	77	80	80	80	=	317
F. Collins	77	85	79	77	=	318
A. Herd	73	81	84	80	=	318
Mr. J. Graham	77	79	81	81	=	318

1924 Open — Walter Hagen

Walter Hagen

The British Open was scheduled for June 26th and 27th on the Royal Liverpool links at Hoylake. When we arrived the same old weather prevailed ... the typical piercing, quick-shifting winds off the sea, cool but not unpleasantly so. As at Troon the year before I barely managed to qualify, but this time I almost lost out before ever posting a score.

Jim Barnes and I were due to qualify on the second day at Formby about forty minutes down from Liverpool, but we arrived ten minutes late. The committee put up quite a fuss. The result of their argument was that they agreed to let me play but to bar Jim. We had a legitimate excuse, a late train; how they arrived at such a crazy decision I'll never know. Of course, we could have put up a tent and camped out on the course the night before in the chilly wind![1]

On my first qualifying round I shot 83, but I made the second in a sizzling 73. Other American pros to qualify included MacDonald Smith, Gil Nicholls and Gene Sarazen. In that second qualifying round I'd been playing the fourth hole, a blind one — British course officials have an attendant ring a bell when the forward players are off the green on these blind holes — and I'd been waiting and waiting for the bell to announce that the pair in front had finished. I told my caddie, "It may take me a long time to ring that bell, too." We finally got the signal and I hit my shot over the direction marker set up to give the players the line to the hole. We then walked down to the green to find my ball in the cup. That eagle right there was the margin which let me qualify. Those two close years of barely scraping by resulted in my taking qualifying a bit more seriously in the years to follow.

I was sincerely pleased when the committee informed me that Mr. John Ball was entering his last British Open and had requested that he be paired with me, Walter *High*gen.[2] I went over immediately to assure him I'd be very honoured to play with him. "Uncle John" was a legend in British golf. He had competed in his first Open at the age of fifteen in 1876 and had finished sixth. Between 1888 and 1912 he won the British Amateur title eight times and in 1890 he became the first British amateur ever to win the British Open. Now at the age of sixty-three he was right there shooting for another win. He was playing in his last Championship on the very course where his father's hotel had been located when "Uncle John" began his golfing career. In fact, the course was laid out on the grounds where his father had originally raced fine horses.

My start was not sensational, for I took a 77 for the first round in the championship. But on the second I finished in 73 to stand three stokes back of the

[1] The story of Jim Barnes disqualification is puzzling. From newspapers and draw sheet, it appears that he did qualify, but despite a score of 155 in the first two rounds he did not play in the last two. Was that when he was disqualified?

[2] Hagen did indeed play with John Ball, but this was in a practice round, when he played the best ball of three amateurs.

leader, Ernie Whitcombe, one of the three famous golfing brothers, and one stroke back of J.H. Taylor. MacDonald Smith and I were tied at 150. On my third round the next day I had a 74 and Ernie Whitcombe and I entered the final round on even terms.

Walter Hagen pitching to the 8th

There had certainly been a clearing of the decks from the close play of the previous day. Arthur Havers, the defending champion who had beaten me by one shot in 1923, came to grief with his third round of 80. Abe Mitchell, playing with Arnaud Massy, was spraying his shots wildly and they both gave up at the fourteenth hole and straggled back to the locker-room. Mac Smith seemed a good bet to take the lead but his third round of 77 put him three shots back of me. On his final round he finished with a 77 giving him a 304 for a tie with Frank Ball for third. J.H. Taylor, the great warrior who had won five British Championships, soared to 79 on his third round, leaving him four shots behind me going to the final round. His last round of 79 gave him a total of 307.

I went out in the final round in 41, two better than Whitcombe, but way over what I'd hoped to shoot. At the twelfth hole Johnny Farrell, who had come over to play in the Open but didn't get the chance because a wasp stung him on the thumb, came out to tell me that Ernie had finished his round and turned in a 301.

"What are you doing?" Johnny asked.

"I've got to finish in par to tie him," I said.

I'd already played my second shot and my third was a difficult niblick shot just over the trap. The hole was hidden behind the trap.

"I'm going to take a chance right here," I told Johnny. "I've got to cut this just right. If it stops right, I can hole it for a 4." It did.

On the thirteenth I thought, since I'd got the twelfth out of the way, the rest shouldn't be too difficult, but the wind had grown to gale strength and there were three long holes ahead of me. The wind was at my back at the thirteenth — a short hole — but I misjudged the force of it and put my ball right in a trap. However, I made a great recovery shot for a 3.

The fourteenth is a par 5, a dogleg, and here the wind was with me for I got a good tee shot over and across the heavy rough and made my par. At the fifteenth I had to cut straight into the teeth of the wind ... two long difficult shots to the green. I was now the only one left on the course who had a chance to tie with or beat Whitcombe. This was the first time Britain had charged admission, and more than ten thousand paying customers surrounded the green.

I elected to play a driver shot quail-high for my second. This particular driver was a new club. I'd had it made and was crazy about it, but somehow I hadn't been able to make it work for me. As I hesitated for a moment and realised I couldn't reach the green with a brassie, I decided to use a club in which I had little or no confidence. I felt I couldn't expect too much from the driver and perhaps that made me concentrate particularly effectively on making the best possible stroke. Anyhow, the ball stopped fifteen feet from the hole. I missed the putt but was mighty happy with my par 4.

On the par 5 dogleg sixteenth, aided by a favourable wind, I hit my second shot over a huge dyke which extends out into the fairway, and which is out of bounds. It was a beautiful brassie shot and let me reach the green in two. But here I lost the one-stroke advantage over par which I seemed to have gained, for I three-putted. This is one of the few times I three-putted.

At the seventeenth — a hole which gave everybody trouble during the Championship, including me — I was straight back against the wind again. Playing this hole right meant placing the tee shot close to the rough on the right side of the fairway, to get a more open shot at the hole. The hole itself was guarded by a series of traps running diagonally in front of the green. It was a very treacherous green because you could quite easily hit your second shot too strongly and go through a fence which bounded the back edge of the green. I played a good shot that carried the traps and held the green, stopping eighteen feet from the hole. I hit an almost perfect putt, too, but a bit too hard and the ball hit the cup and jumped out. I got my par 4.

At the eighteenth I was confident I had victory in the palm of my hand, for here was a short par-4 hole with the wind at my back. I got a long tee shot, some 300 yards, leaving me a short seven-iron shot for my second. Again a series of traps crossed the front of the green. However, they didn't seem to be too troublesome considering the shortness of the shot I had to make.

I played my second shot too boldly and went past the flag to the back edge of the green. Here I was on this fast green ... on the back edge at that ... and I needed to get down in two. I putted down, sloping away, and left myself five feet short. Had I hit it a tiny bit harder I would have rolled almost to the hole. But a semi-circular ridge held my ball and left me with a most difficult putt.

With such a fast green I knew my stroke must be delicate. I looked over both sides of the hole. There was a slim chance of a slight roll as it went down a little incline towards the hole. I studied it carefully once more. I decided there was a double roll down the first two feet of the putt to the right, a slight roll to the left the last two feet. I stood and set myself with one thing uppermost in my mind.

I must hit the ball delicately. And in a situation like this delicacy is difficult due to the extreme nervous tension one is under. But then I had a second thought which helped greatly in my executing the shot correctly and in not being over-anxious to see where the ball was going. Should I miss, I'd only need to stay over another day to beat Whitcombe in the play-off of the British Championship. If I holed, I became the British Open champion.

While ten thousand people held their breath, I stroked the ball ... gently but firmly; it righted the last turn, straightened out and headed for home! I threw my putter into the air and never saw the ball or the putter again. But I sure saw that British Open trophy!

(from *The Walter Hagen Story* published by Heinemann 1957)

LEADING SCORES

Walter Hagen	77	73	74	77	=	301
E.R. Whitcombe	77	70	77	78	=	302
F. Ball	78	75	74	77	=	304
MacDonald Smith	76	74	77	77	-	304
J.H. Taylor	75	74	79	79	-	307
L. Holland	74	78	78	78	=	308
Aubrey Boomer	75	78	76	79	=	308
George Duncan	74	79	74	81	=	308
J.M. Barber	78	77	79	75	=	309
G. Gadd	79	75	78	77	=	309
P.F. Weston	76	77	77	79	=	309
J.G. Sherlock	76	75	78	80	=	309

1930 Open — Bobby Jones

Robert T. Jones

Editors' note: Bobby Jones had already triumphed in the Amateur Championship at St. Andrews when he came to Hoylake for the Open Championship. Though he qualified with something to spare, his play in the two rounds at Wallasey and Hoylake had been only moderate; following his second round one writer was prompted to say that he "took a turn among the ordinary mortals by compiling a score of 77".

Next day, however, was the first round of the tournament proper, and at its conclusion I found myself with a score of seventy, tied for the lead with Henry Cotton and MacDonald Smith.

I remember being somewhat startled late that afternoon upon returning to Liverpool, where we were staying at the Adelphi Hotel, to see a banner headline in an afternoon paper, "Eight Inches Off a World's Record". To my surprise I found that the headline was related to the round I had played that day. I confess that I had some difficulty appreciating the relevance of it.

To be sure, I had accomplished a very satisfactory round. After the first three holes my shots to the green had been reasonably good, and my putting had been of the kind that at least made for comfort, if not for a very low score. With my first putt I was always leaving the ball so that, as Keeler liked to describe it, "You could cover the ball and the hole with a derby hat." As a consequence I had not had to go through any agonising struggles with the three- and four-footers. But I had been grateful that I had only had to tap in so many putts for pars, rather than being disappointed, as the British headline had suggested, that more of the longer putts had not gone in.

Hoylake has always been a long, testing course, but singularly lacking in subtleties. I think it could be said to be a long hitter's paradise, because, although the distances are considerable, the ground, on the whole, is quite flat. The entire course is there for the player to see, and I should think that the first time around he ought to know as much about it as he could ever learn.

In some strange way, though, my experience with the course seemed to be precisely opposite to that of my fellow competitors. I seemed to have my trouble where everyone else was holding his own or building up a cushion, and contrarily, I managed to make my hay on the holes that caused others the most trouble.

The first three holes at Hoylake were good holes, but of no extraordinary difficulty. The first two were par fours of moderate length, while the third, of something like 480 yards, could be called a par five, but was in reality easily reachable in two shots. Yet in the first three rounds, the total of my scores on these three holes, played three times, came to a matter of eight strokes over an average of fours. In effect, I had in every round, except the last, hung a weight around my neck before I had fairly got started.

The last five holes at Hoylake averaged over 450 yards, with two of them over the 500 mark. This was at that time reputed to be the most difficult finishing stretch in the world. Others had their trials with it, but for me the contrariness continued, and in every round except one I managed to improve on the card on these holes. Yet because of the first three, every round of this tournament was a struggle.

The second day I added a seventy-two to the seventy of the first round, so that at the half-way point I was leading the field, although only by one stroke over Fred Robson and three over Horton Smith. I had a margin of five over Compston, who had played so well in the qualifying.

Five strokes sounds like an awful lot, but here is what can happen. On the morning of the final day I began my third round 4,5,6, and Compston, starting about an hour later, did these first three holes in 4,3,4, and then added a 2 at the short fourth, where I had taken a par 3. In four holes, my lead of five strokes had vanished completely.

Beginning with the fourth hole, I had managed to settle down and had played the next ten holes with five fours and five threes, so that three over-fours had now become two under, and the prospect of seventy-one or seventy-two for the round quite reasonable.

I can't say whether it had any effect or not, but I do have a very vivid recollection that all during the latter half of that round the cheers from Compston's gallery were ringing in my ears. The American domination of the British Open had been unbroken for a number of years, and it was quite natural that a British crowd should lustily cheer Compston's great play. They must have been confident that the long drought was about to be broken.

In any event the final five holes, which had been so good to me up to this point, for the first time caused me trouble. This time I needed four fives in the stretch of five, and so turned my seventy-one or seventy-two into a seventy-four.

I thought I had done pretty well starting home 3,3,4,3, but Compston went 3,3,3,2, and finished in sixty-eight to take the lead from me by a stroke at 215 to 216.

I can still see the awesome figure made by Compston towards the finish of his round. One of the British writers said that he was playing "like a frenzied giant". A tall, powerful man, Compston was truly striding after the ball as though he could not wait to vent his fury upon it. Watching from the clubhouse as I saw him sweep past the sixteenth green, I had the feeling that spectators, tee-boxes, benches, even, might be swirled up into his wake. As he left the eighteenth green after this great sixty-eight and made his beaming way to the clubhouse through a myriad of well-wishers, he was about as happy a figure as I have ever seen. At the time I was heading for the first tee to start my final round.

Never, it seemed, at least during that year, was it to be given to me simply to play an ordinary round of golf and then wait to see whether or not it would be good enough. Things just could not be that simple.

Yet it did seem a good omen when I managed for the first time to get past the opening holes in decent figures, especially so, perhaps, because of one outrageous piece of good fortune.

After an uneventful four at the first hole, I hit a high towering drive off the second tee, which I saw coming down a yard or two off the right edge of the fairway into the heavy rough. As I watched the ball descending, I also saw that it was going to land very close to one of the gallery stewards wearing his identifying red skull-cap. I have often wondered what that fellow's head had been made of. He was in no wise injured by the impact, but my ball, landing on his head, careered some fifty yards entirely across an adjoining fairway, and finished in a bunker intended to be a hazard for players approaching the fourteenth green. I am unable to say whether or not the accident resulted in my ball being nearer the hole than it would otherwise have been. I do know that it found a very clean lie in the sand which was infinitely preferable to one in the deep rough for which it had been headed.

This second shot from the sand was almost exactly the same shot I had holed on the fourth hole at St. Andrews in the match against Sid Roper. I played the same club and, as nearly as possible, the same shot. This one did not hole out, but it finished about twenty feet from the hole, after which I holed the putt for a birdie three. It was a most auspicious start for the last round.

Having this time safely passed the early holes, I continued on a very comfortable way until I arrived at the eighth tee, needing two fours, which were entirely reasonable, in order to be out in thirty-five. This was the best I had done to this point during the tournament, and I must admit that I was feeling most optimistic. I felt that Compston must inevitably suffer some reaction from his great round of the morning (actually he put himself completely out with an eighty-two), and no one else was close enough to offer serious challenge if I could but put in a reasonably good round.

The eighth hole at Hoylake was of some 480 yards, but I had been consistently either on, or just off, the green in two shots. This time was no exception. After a good drive my spoon second just missed the left edge of the green and rolled off some ten or fifteen yards down an innocent slope. It lay still in the fairway with absolutely nothing between it and the flag.

Bobby Jones driving to the 8th

The events of the next few moments caused much wonderment among the spectators and golfing authorities present. Mr. Darwin said later that a nice old lady with a croquet mallet could have saved me two strokes from this point. Yet I will swear that I took seven on that hole in the most reasonable manner possible.

First, to describe the situation. My ball lay some ten or fifteen yards off the putting surface. The hole was located another five yards, perhaps, beyond the edge of the green. From the ball the fairway sloped upwards to the putting surface, and then dropped off in a fairly fast slope to the hole and beyond. The green was quite keen.

I felt that I had done quite well up to this point. I wanted desperately to get that four so that I could take things a bit more easily from that point on. I tried to let my first chip die just on to the edge of the green, hoping that it would roll down close to the hole. I was not willing to play conservatively past the hole with the idea of settling for a five.

The first chip was underplayed and did not quite reach the putting surface. Still, with the same respect for the keen green, I left the second chip some ten feet short of the hole. Trying very hard to save a par at least, I slipped the first putt a foot past the hole, and then, a bit unsettled perhaps, hurriedly tapped the next one — and it didn't go in.

The whole thing was at once so unbelievable, and yet so supremely simple, that it comprised the most perfect example of the potentialities of torment ever-present for the contestant in an Open Championship. I have had a number of such experiences, yet never one which I had any reason whatever to anticipate. Always, it has been possible to look back and to see how they have happened without the commission of any real atrocities. Almost always, they have resulted from a succession of strokes which have not been quite precisely played, plus a tiny relaxation of concentration, or perhaps a little carelessness or petulance.

However possible it may be to rationalize or minimize the occurrence, it is certainly not possible to exaggerate its impact upon the player. As I walked to the ninth tee, I was in a daze. I realized that in one brief span of only a moment or two, all the effort of the past three days had been just about washed out. I wasn't looking at any Grand Slam, only at the one championship. If ever a person could be made groggy by a blow entailing no physical consequences, I had been made so by that seven.

I should like to say that this disaster caused me to rise up in all my might and resolve to win out at all costs. I should like to feel that from that point on it was my blazing spirit that carried me on to victory. The fact is, though, that I did anything but that.

My reaction was precisely this. I had been badly shaken and I knew it. I was even confused mentally. At this point I was completely incapable of making any calculation either of what score I might ultimately achieve or of what it would be necessary to do to stave off the challenge of others. Since I could not think, I did what I think nine persons out of ten would have done in similar circumstances. I simply resolved to keep on hitting the ball as best I could, to finish the round in an orderly fashion, if possible, and let the result be what it would. I had no more thought of attacking or defending or of being over par or under par, but merely of finishing.

Only one stroke of all the rest has left any definite impression. I know that I did the next five holes in four each, but two of them were par threes. And then I faced those five long finishing holes.

I remember getting a four at the fourteenth. At the fifteenth I played my second a bit short of the green, chipped up to within a half-dozen feet, and missed the putt. And so to the sixteenth, which produced a shot that was one of the best I ever made in my life. As it turned out, it won the championship for me.

The sixteenth hole at Hoylake in 1930 was 532 yards in length. It was a dog-leg to the right around the corner of a dyke, at about 270 yards from the tee. The green was wide and flat, and whatever may have been on the right-hand side, there was a bunker at the left-front corner of the green. Going all-out for a four, which I knew I needed desperately, my long wood second was pulled just enough to finish in this left-hand bunker.

When I reached my ball, I found it lying cleanly on the smooth sand, but very close to the left-hand wall of the bunker — that is, the wall on the side opposite the hole.

The slope of this wall was quite abrupt, so that there could be no thought of playing any ordinary blast or half-blast, or even a chip. The ball could only be struck by a sharply descending blow, and my right foot had to be placed almost at the top of the bank behind me. The hole lay at some twenty to twenty-five yards across the flat, shining green.

I had not used for any important shot during the whole year the massive, concave sand-wedge which Horton Smith had given me earlier in the year. At St. Andrews I had hacked a ball out of a gorse-bush with it, and in this tournament at Hoylake I had used it for a routine shot on the first hole in one of the earlier rounds. But as I looked at this situation on the seventieth hole of the championship, I could see that this was the only club with which this shot could be played successfully. If I could drop the club behind the ball so that contact would be made just above centre of the face of the club, the loft should be just about right to play a running shot across the green. I knew it was dangerous to use a club with which I had so little familiarity, but it was the only hope. The shot came off precisely as intended, the ball popped over the forward bank of the bunker and crept slowly across the green until it tickled the edge of the hole and stopped two inches beyond.

That did it. I had to hole a reasonable putt for a four at the seventeenth. But I finished with another four at the eighteenth and was safe from pursuit. Leo Diegel, coming along an hour later, took six at this same sixteenth hole and so lost to me by two strokes. Macdonald Smith, just as happened later in the American Championship, needed a two at the par-four eighteenth to tie me. The par four, which he got, left him tied with Diegel for second.

These last two British championships were the hardest ones of any I could remember. I might say they still are.

(from *Golf Is My Game* published by Chatto & Windus 1961)

LEADING SCORES

Mr. R.T. Jones	70	72	74	75	=	291
Leo Diegel	74	73	71	75	=	293
MacDonald Smith	70	77	75	71	=	293
Horton Smith	72	73	78	73	=	296
F. Robson	71	72	78	75	=	296
J. Barnes	71	77	72	77	=	297
A. Compston	74	73	68	82	=	297
Henry Cotton	70	79	77	73	=	299
T. Barber	75	76	72	77	=	300
A. Boyer	73	77	70	80	=	300
C.A. Whitcombe	74	75	72	79	=	300
B. Hodson	74	77	76	74	=	301

1936 Open — Alfred Padgham

Edward Birchall

A flurry of controversy attended the 1936 Open.

The use of new back tees on more than half the holes had extended the Links to what one commentator described as "the almost monstrous length" of 7,078 yards. Golf was becoming a test of endurance, wrote another critic. Before the qualifying rounds began, the previous year's winner, Alfred Perry said the course was too severe, but the best man would win.

The attitude of the Club in making the new teeing grounds, which stretched the course so far as to make a man walk six miles in every round, was clearly outlined by the then Club Secretary, Major H.C. Forbes-Bell.

"Our object all along has been to produce the best golfer of the year, — that is all. We are not in the least concerned with what score he will do. First class golf should be a matter of accuracy as well as length. Under modern conditions, unless you stretch your course length is bound to predominate. These men hit the ball so far that the original bunkers no longer come into play and they can get the greens with their second shots wherever their drives finish. They can play one bad shot and still get their 4 — and that is what we have tried to stop. We want them to play four good shots out of four. We regard ourselves as being on trial."

Hoylake triumphantly survived the test and the winning score of 287 was the lowest recorded in an Open Championship up to that time.

The winner was Alfred H. Padgham, professional at Sundridge Park, Kent. "He was the right man to win, everybody rejoiced to see him do it," wrote Bernard Darwin in *The Times*, adding that he had done it over probably the longest, sternest course that had ever tested a golfer.

Alfred Padgham

Padgham is said to have owed his win to his gloriously tranquil and unruffled temperament rather than to his great and unquestionable skill. It may have seemed absurd to say of a man who did such a score over such a course that he did not play his best game but it is claimed as the cold truth that Padgham had often played better in the sense of making fewer mistakes. He showed his really heroic quality by the character of his recoveries.

If he was not on the green in 2, he chipped dead; if he was not dead he holed the putt — sometimes a very long putt. In particular when everyone else faded a little over the last five holes, Padgham went from strength to strength. Other people were four under 4s with five to play and Padgham was only one under, but it was Padgham who finished best. The Field, the Lake, the Dun, the Royal and the Stand, those five great holes met only one master and he was rightly Open Champion.

The first round left Padgham, Henry Cotton, and Gene Sarazen, the three main favourites, level at 73, three strokes behind Bill Cox and two behind James Adams. Padgham's first nine holes had provided a model of consistency, for he had nine 4s in a row. About seven of them there was little to be said except that he played patiently and holed a good putt at the Long. His 4 at the Cop was due, apparently, to underclubbing; at any rate he was short of the bunker which is where bad players finish when they miss the shot. At the Dowie, by way of contrast, he went too far into the hollow beyond the green.

Coming home Padgham did allow 5s to creep in, one at the Dee, another at the Field and another, rather gratuitously, at the home hole, where he laid a lovely chip nearly dead from the back of the green and then missed what an onlooker might have termed "a silly little putt".

Padgham's second round was well worth watching, since it aroused almost all the emotions that golf can produce — awe, disappointment, pity and ecstatic admiration, one after the other.

The first seven holes were awe-inspiring. Every shot was hit perfectly and better than perfectly played. There was just a perceptible breeze when he started, so that he had to take wood for his second to the first hole and could not quite reach the green at the Long with two glorious hits. Yet he had the first seven holes in two under 4s, without holing a single putt of more than negligible length. Then came a bad time. A 5 at the eighth, was forgiveable, but another at the Punchbowl meant a real loss of a stroke. Then he was bunkered off the tee at the Dee and a third successive 5 seemed inevitable but Padgham, walking up to his ball on the green with his same slow stride, holed a beast of a bending putt of fully five yards and got his 4 after all. He had a thoroughly bad 6 at the Hilbre, without touching sand, and then took a 5 at the Field, where he was in the rough all the way.

That was one over 4s with four terrific holes to play and there was much shaking of heads but this was the kind of situation that found this "superbly sleepy golfer" at his best. He got a good 4 at the Lake and a distinctly lucky 4 at the Dun, where he hooked into the rough from the tee, played a third otherwise than intended and then holed a long putt. His 4 at the Royal was perfectly orthodox and at the Stand he holed a putt variously estimated in yards, but unquestionably long. With two rounds completed, Padgham was one stroke behind Adams and Cox, both of whom returned 144. Henry Cotton was one of four more on Padgham's figure of 145.

The final day opened with a shock for Padgham. He was playing early and had left his clubs in the Professional's shop overnight. It was firmly locked and it seemed as though he would have to use borrowed clubs. However, he decided on direct action. He broke a window of the shop, clambered in and rescued his clubs, including the precious putter, in the nick of time. He then proceeded to go round in 71. This was the round of a great player with an ideal temperament rather than a great round. He did not look really comfortable, which was not surprising considering his act of burglary! He was inclined to hook shots and had to rely too much on his putter. He did not rely in vain for he holed some desperately good ones, and these plus his power of doing 4s at the last five holes, where weaker men take 5s, pulled him through. So he set up a mark of 216 for three rounds — "Good enough in all conscience" in the judgement of Mr. Darwin but, as it turned out, a stroke behind Adams and Cotton.

Long before most people had begun to think of luncheon, Padgham was away for his final round and his beginning was not of a very high promise, for he was bunkered off his second tee shot and had hard work to get his 5. The third cost him a 5 as well, no great hindrance may be, but assuredly no help. A great burst of 3,4,4, for the Dowie, Far and Punchbowl brought him to the turn in 37 but that was hardly good enough.

The first few homeward holes at Hoylake are crucial and Padgham holed them superbly in 4,3,4,2. So he came to that tremendous finish that never betrayed him and began auspiciously with a 4 at the Field. Two 5s running crept in but he had his 4 at the Royal with a lovely approach and at the last he holed a putt of several yards for a 3. As the ball dropped spectators had the feeling that had done it.

Joe Ezar, the American trick golfer, had also finished early. He had looked on the board and saw that it would be about two hours before the next real contenders, Cotton and Sarazen, would be finishing, and he went up to the front balcony and announced to spectators around the Clubhouse that he would give a trick shot exhibition in the practice ground. Quite a crowd followed him over. When he had finished he passed the hat round and rumour had it that he collected a sum not far short of the £100 prize money received by the winner.

Padgham, too, could have entertained the assembled crowd, but not at golf. He was an accomplished motor cycle trick rider, and used to perform hair raising stunts at fairs and similar functions. Only his father approved. It was obvious to other members of the family that this sideline was not without danger, and could jeopardize his career as a golfer. His uncle's efforts to get it stopped met with a blunt negative response and caused a lasting family rift. On this occasion Padgham could only wait, first for Adams, who missed a putt on the last green to tie, and then for Cotton who could do no better than 74, two shots too many.

So once again Hoylake had produced a worthy Champion.

But what of the course and the Club? Firstly Henry Longhurst commented "The people who were responsible for the new course were assailed with much criticism, written and spoken, long before the Championship began. The course, it was said, was too long, the players would never get round it; golf was becoming a matter of endurance and so forth. To all of which the reply was 'wait and see'. We waited, we saw, and we were conquered. Hoylake, as it played during the Championship week, turned out to be the finest test of golf in the world. So many persons, whose opinions are entitled to respect, were agreed on the point that such a statement ceases to be dogmatic. Gene Sarazen, who has travelled all over the world in pursuit of golf, remarked time and time again, 'it is the greatest course I have ever seen'."

Secondly Bernard Darwin wrote "If ever a course was in great order, it was Hoylake. As to the management of it, that may be taken as read. Hoylake knows its business."

LEADING SCORES

A.H. Padgham	73	72	71	71	=	287
J. Adams	71	73	71	73	=	288
M. Dallemagne	73	72	75	69	=	289
Henry Cotton	73	72	70	74	=	289
Gene Sarazen	73	75	70	73	=	291
T. Green	74	72	70	75	=	291
Percy Alliss	74	72	74	71	=	291
R.A. Whitcombe	72	77	71	74	=	294
Mr. A.D. Locke	75	73	72	74	=	294
A.J. Lacey	76	74	72	72	=	294
D.J. Rees	77	71	72	75	=	295
R. Burton	74	71	75	76	=	296
W.J. Cox	70	74	79	73	=	296

1947 Open — Fred Daly

John Behrend

After the war the Championship was soon back at Hoylake. The links had certainly not suffered from the five years' lack of attention, and The Times correspondent described the greens as "lovely, of a comfortable easy pace" and "the whole course a miracle of velvety smoothness".

The 1947 Open will not be remembered for one of the strongest fields. Sam Snead, Champion of 1946, did not return to defend his title, and the American challenge was thin, but all the top home players were there, and a few other overseas men of stature, notably Norman von Nida who was to lead the qualifers and Flory van Donck. What will be remembered is the excitement of the final round. Four men were tying for the lead and another half dozen or so were in contention.

Fred Daly was four shots ahead after 36 holes with rounds of 73 and 70. Henry Cotton who had started a firm favourite, as he normally did in Championships at that time, had led with a splendid 69 in the first round, but had started the second 5,5,6 and had slumped to 78. Despite that, he was lying second equal with Sam King. Laurie Ayton, who had also had a first round 69 took two more than Cotton. But on the final morning Daly, who in the second round had been "playing every conceivable and inconceivable chip dead", came back to the field with a 78. He had no major disaster; the shots just slipped away over the last nine holes.

Many of the early starters, Daly included, were on their way in the fourth round long before those at the end of the field had finished their morning round.

Though the position for spectators would not have emerged with such clarity, the scores after three rounds were as follows:

T.H. Cotton	221
A. Lees	221
N.G. von Nida	221
F. Daly	221
Mr. F.R. Stranahan	222
R.A. Whitcombe	223
R.W. Horne	223
L.B. Ayton	223
A. Perry	223

It was one from outside this group that set the target. Bill Shankland was six under 4s with five holes left to play, but the Hoylake finish took its toll and he could do no better than 70 for 295. Reg Horne, just behind him, beat that by a single shot; if only his second to the 16th had held its line and not fallen into the bunker guarding the front left of the green, as the quality of the stroke deserved, he might have been putting for a 3 and not settling for his 5. And if only his putt at the 18th hadn't stopped on the lip, he might well have put himself in an unassailable position.

Daly at the 4th tee

Daly had taken 38 to the turn, but started for home with two 3s and a 4. The 13th had not been kind to him. Twice already he had three-putted there. This time he played a disastrous tee shot into the pit fifty yards or so in front of the tee. From there he could only extricate it to the edge of the green, but the damage was quickly repaired with a putt of some twenty yards up the green and into the hole. Inspired by this he got his 4s at the Field, the Lake and the Dun. Now he could afford to drop a shot and still beat Horne — but he dropped two shots at the 17th with a tentative pitch and 3 putts. So he needed a 4 to tie. A good second left him some 12 yards from the pin and, to the delight of the large Irish contingent present, he holed it. As he left the green amidst the cheering, his fans tried to lift him shoulder high and chair him to the Clubhouse. But Daly would have none of it. There were still several players out on the course with a chance, even though the wind was freshening.

Cotton had reached the turn in 36, but with a 6 at the 10th the initiative was gone and he struggled home in 40. Von Nida had taken 39 to the turn and he too finished with a 76 as did Arthur Lees. Realistically there was no one else, as Stranahan, the powerful American amateur, playing at the end of the field needed to come home in 33 to tie. Yet as he stood on the 16th tee, he could still do it with two 4s and a 3. He got his 4 at the Dun, was on the Royal green for 2, went for the putt and missed the return. That was it. The press men who had already phoned through their copy, could breathe a sigh of relief. But Stranahan had not given up. Having hit an enormous drive at the final hole he walked forward the 100 yards or so to the green to check the exact location of the pin, then back to the ball; after some further thought, he selected his club and played the stroke. It pitched on the green on line for the hole and ran slowly forward, missing the hole and a tie by the merest whisker.

So after that anxious two hour wait Fred Daly became the first Irishman to have his name on the trophy, and a very worthy name it proved to be, as in the next five Open Championships he was to finish second once, third twice and fourth once. Daly, then aged 35, was no great stylist, but he whistled and waggled his way round, keeping the ball in play and pitching and putting as well as anyone. As to his waggling he was asked how many he normally had. "I waggle until I'm good and ready" he answered.

Frank Stranahan

Forty years later Fred was back at Hoylake with his friends from the Belfast press to receive Honorary Life Membership of the Royal Liverpool Golf Club. Tony Colvin, the Captain, told Fred that he looked "just the same — a little more mature perhaps" and Fred, now a good deal less tongue-tied than he had been at the Championship Presentation, entered into the spirit by giving his solution to the raging controversy of the time — what should happen to the Dowie: "It's a great hole — just make a pond on the left and put some crocodiles in it."

Fred has been back again with his friends from Portrush and has presented a trophy for annual competition between the two Clubs. He has also donated to the Club his Letters prototype wedge, which, with its now illegal punched face markings, played many of the "conceivable and inconceivable chips." He can't quite remember whether that was the club that extricated him from the pit at the 13th. Whether or not, it stands proudly in the showcase as a reminder of one of Hoylake's favourite Champions.

LEADING SCORES

F. Daly	73	70	78	72	=	293
Mr. Frank Stranahan	71	79	72	72	=	294
R.W. Horne	77	74	72	71	=	294
W. Shankland	76	74	75	70	=	295
R. Burton	77	71	77	71	=	296
J. Bulla	80	72	74	71	=	297
C.H. Ward	76	73	76	72	=	297
S.L. King	75	72	77	73	=	297
A. Lees	75	74	72	76	=	297
N.G. von Nida	74	76	71	76	=	297
Henry Cotton	69	78	74	76	=	297
J. Adams	73	80	71	75	=	299
A.H. Padgham	75	75	74	76	=	300
R.A. Whitcombe	75	77	71	77	=	300

SOME PERSONAL MEMORIES

Fred Daly

Forty-two years on, and still people never tire of asking me about the Open victory at Royal Liverpool. Not just in Ireland, but everywhere I go.

"Tell us again Fred. What was it really like? How did you feel?"

More often than not, the inquisitors were not even born the day I raised that famous claret jug in triumph all those years ago.

I adore Hoylake. It's a marvellous course, which can provide a fearsome test particularly when the wind gets up.

I was made a life member during Tony Colvin's captaincy on a wonderful summer's night at the club a few years ago. The sense of tradition and companionship I feel everytime I return to that little corner of Merseyside, is overwhelming — and yet a far cry from the reception I received when I first turned up at the front door of the clubhouse in 1947. Dear me, what a frosty welcome.

Harry Bradshaw from Portmarnock and myself, who had just travelled over from Manchester, presented ourselves for accreditation. My recollection of what we were told is somewhat blurred now, but it went something like this:

Commissionaire — "Sorry we've no tickets, so please be off — both of you".

It was a humiliating experience. We felt like a couple of Irish navvies grubbing around for some labouring work. Old Cyril Hughes, the professional then took us out for a round, and not long after we finished, Commander Roe, secretary of the PGA at the time, and a lovely man, quickly sorted out the confusion. I laugh now, but at the time it wasn't so funny, and quite frankly, somewhat unsettling before such an important tournament.

Needless to say Harry and I were soon afforded all the necessary facilities, and of course everyone knows the sequel.

I have to admit that I felt overawed by the international company I was keeping when I stepped onto the first tee, but inside I honestly believed I could beat Cotton and the rest — and no, Daly simply wasn't there to make up the numbers.

The American Frank Stranahan chased me hard, and his penultimate shot of the tournament is still recalled on this side of the Irish sea. A nine iron right to the heart of the 18th, and eight inches from the hole — or was it?

At the time I was in the bar with the Whitcombe brothers, Reg and Ernie, quietly confident of pocketing the winner's cheque, unaware and unconcerned about the drama unfolding outside. Stranahan needed a par, birdie finish to force a tie, but bogied the 17th, before striking that second, 150 yards to the final green. One of the Sunday colour supplements this year posed the question: "Was this one of the 10 best golf shots ever?"

I will withhold judgement. That shot has been the subject of so much comment and speculation, that as each year passes, it seems to me that Frank's ball is still inching towards the hole. It's amazing the way distances change in the mists of time.

Somebody insisted it was eight inches. "No, no it was six," I heard someone say. Somebody else argued: "Listen, it was less than three. I know, because I was there."

And so the debate goes on.

In fact I have this recurring nightmare which goes something like this: A voice at the other end of the telephone exclaims: "Fred, you are never going to believe this, but Stranahan really did hole that nine iron. Could you dig out the clubs again and get over here for a play-off?"

1956 Open — Peter Thomson

John Graham

It was my great fortune to be Captain of Hoylake in 1956. Not only was the Club host to the News of the World Professional Match Play Championship but it was also host to the Open Championship. Two important Championships in one year were quite beyond the dreams of a forty-one year old member. The real work had been done by the previous Captain — John Postlethwaite and his Committees — and all I had to do was to enjoy the fruits of their considerable labour and, very unfairly, take the credit. My main job was to entertain the important officials in the world of golf. I found myself mixing with people whose names were well-known in golfing circles. One of these was Henry Cotton.

The Royal Liverpool Golf Club does not bestow nicknames on its members lightly. Among the few, I recall, are "The Chieftain", who was Robert Wilson, "Pendulum" Brown and a brace of "Crows" (Guy Farrar and Peter Crosthwaite). But the one I knew best was "Henry Cotton" — not, of course, the Henry Cotton, but one Eric Langdon. He idolised the great man. If Henry Cotton wore a certain type of pullover, trousers or shoes, then within the week Eric would be sporting the same. Whenever he could, he followed the Maestro and in whatever Championship or event he entered, there was no one else in it so far as Eric was concerned. Members of the Club knew him better as "Henry Cotton" than as Eric Langdon.

Before the Open some of the Professionals arrived a couple of days or so early to get a little extra practice. Driving-off times were shared with the members. On one of these days I had arranged to play at 2.20 pm with a member, Arthur Jones, who had asked me to find someone to join us. At about one o'clock I was looking out of the Club window, when I espied a solitary figure in the Practice Field. To my astonishment it was the Maestro himself, Henry Cotton, hitting shots into the distance. I went out to watch him. Henry always did his homework. He always knew who was the Captain, the Chairman of the Green Committee and the Green-keeper. After two or three shots with an iron, he astounded me by asking if I would like to play a few holes with him. I told him about Arthur Jones and he said: "I will play your best ball."

Henry Cotton — 5th tee

2.20 pm duly came and I was on the tee. Arthur Jones arrived and asked me if I had fixed up with anyone. I replied "Yes, Henry Cotton"; Arthur immediately thought that I meant Eric Langdon. The Maestro then appeared round the corner and I watched the incredulous look on the face of Arthur Jones when he began to realise that it was not Eric Langdon, but the real thing. It was a minute or two before he recovered.

We set off with Henry in an expansive mood. He chatted freely, gave us some hints and told a number of stories. When we had reached the seventh hole, we were thoroughly enjoying ourselves. Why shouldn't we? We were three up on the most famous player in the world. But then Toots (Henry's wife) appeared and everything changed. She brought Henry to heel and we were doomed. We were eventually beaten 3 and 2. However, I shall never forget that look on the face of Arthur Jones.

I suppose as Championships go, it was rather a dull one. Gary Player, who was at the beginning of an illustrious career, went round in a record 68 in the qualifying round. The real excitement was in the first round of the Championship proper when Denis Smalldon from Cardiff stood on the sixteenth tee needing three 4s for a 65. He had a shortish putt for his 4 at the sixteenth.Unfortunately at the moment of striking his putt, the television workers at the nearby tower decided to pull up a camera on a pulley. The ensuing noise completely distracted Smalldon, who, not unnaturally, missed his putt and finished with three 5s for a 68. A relieved Guy Farrar, Secretary of the Club, who had been watching these last three holes, returned to the Clubhouse with the knowledge that his beloved Links had not been humbled after all. Henry Cotton finished sixth, but he did not have the best of the weather.

A young Gary Player — finished 4th

I can do no better describing Peter Thomson's win than to quote from Peter Ryde's article in *The Times* of 7th July.

> Yesterday in the suitably historic setting of Royal Liverpool he became the only golfer to win three Open Championships in a row since Bob Ferguson achieved it over two rounds at St. Andrews in 1882 against thirty-nine competitors.
> Since then none of the great golfers from the triumvirate through Jones, Hagen, Cotton and Locke has been able to string three together, and not one of them won his third title at so earlier an age as the present holder. Jones was 28. Thomson will be that next year. Since 1951 when Thomson finished equal sixth he has been second, equal second, and first, first, first. It is indeed his happy hunting ground.
> He has always been the Champion with a perfect temperament, placid and imperturbable, but yesterday from the moment he drove out of bounds at the 6th in the morning it seemed as though the magnitude of the task in hand began to weigh upon him. From there all through that gruelling last round his temperament was put through it as perhaps no other golfer's has been. He certainly held a useful lead, but Van Donck with two splendid rounds of 70 and 74, had reduced Thomson's lead to three strokes at luncheon, and had set a target of 289 for him to beat, which meant a final round of 76. That sounded easy enough but the wind, although less strong, was still a difficult factor.
> Thomson began uncertainly and as the 5s took shape on his card the strain could be felt all round him. He needed to hole a good putt or have some stroke of luck to free him from doubt. The crisis came and went at the 6th and 7th holes of the final round. He had just taken another 5, pitching short into the bunker, and he was left with a 4 foot putt for his 4 at the Briars (6th). He was very deliberate over this and holed it, but a fine tee shot at the Dowie (7th) just ran over the back, and in a painful silence broken only by a small boy banging two tins together, he slipped 6 feet past. This was the putt he had to hole, for if he missed, he might take 39 to the turn and be really up against it. Down it went, and the atmosphere at once became easier.
> From there on doubt faded. He hit a fine second to the back of the 8th green, and what removed all reasonable doubt was that he took his 3s at the Alps (11th) and the Rushes (13th) and so could afford 5s at all but one of the remaining holes. That is nice to know at Hoylake for one never feels quite the same, not, anyway, until one is past the Royal (17th). As it was he needed only two of them, for he chipped close at the 14th and even closer at the 16th. The draw that took him into a left hand bunker at the 17th looked like a safety precaution, then suddenly he was home.

I spent some time watching Thomson win this Championship. He seemed to me to have a totally uncomplicated swing. He was full of confidence in his ability, yet it never appeared in his demeanour. Everything, in fact, looked completely simple. Above all, he was blessed with a wonderful temperament. Luck plays a part in a golfer's life. At Hoylake he had the best of the weather and he took full advantage of it. But, somehow, I felt that if he had played in the worst of it, he would still have won. His marvellous temperament is shown by the following incident. After completing his third round of 72, he had his usual snack, which he always followed by resting. As all the settees and chairs in the Clubhouse were occupied, the Steward, Mr. Greenhill, took him to his private room where, to his amazement, Thomson slept soundly for 30 minutes — a sign of complete relaxation and confidence, which is the hall-mark of a champion.

Peter Thomson — 17th tee

Perhaps I might add a small personal postscript to this Championship. My family has lived in Hoylake for over 100 years. This, let me hastily say, is nothing like as long as many other families. I know a lot of these people. I know what they do, but I do not always know their names. Likewise I am known to some as "the fellow who plays golf", but they probably do not know my name. After the prize giving, I had to pose with the winner giving him the Jug. The next day our pictures appeared in the Press both holding the Jug. A fortnight later I was walking along Market Street in Hoylake when I was stopped by a middle-aged lady who congratulated me on winning the Open Championship. "I saw a picture of you, in the papers, being presented with the Winner's Cup. Well done!"

With that she continued on her way.

I am afraid that I have never told her the truth! But it was a nice way to close my file on the 1956 Open Championship.

LEADING SCORES

P.W. Thomson	70	70	72	74	=	286
F. Van Donck	71	74	70	74	=	289
R. de Vicenzo	71	70	79	70	=	290
Gary Player	71	76	73	71	=	291
J. Panton	74	76	72	70	=	292
Henry Cotton	72	76	71	74	=	293
E. Bertolino	69	72	76	76	=	293
A. Cerda	72	81	68	73	=	294
M. Souchak	74	74	74	72	=	294
C. O'Connor	73	78	74	70	=	295
H. Weetman	72	76	75	72	=	295

1967 Open — Roberto de Vicenzo

Ben Wright

Of one thing I am certain. Not one of the commonly accepted "Big Three" of Arnold Palmer, Jack Nicklaus and Gary Player will be capable of winning the British or any other major Open championship at the age of 44, as did Roberto de Vicenzo here last week. I would not doubt for a minute their indomitable determination to pull off such a feat. In fact, both Nicklaus and Player set new standards of technical application during this wonderful event. But at the risk of being accused of heresy I am sure that none of them possesses a method so sound and simple as does this lovable, bear-like Argentinian. Only such a method could stand up to the strain of 20 years in top-class golf.

De Vicenzo has such immense power in his butcher-sized hands and forearms that he is capable of propelling the golf ball almost 300 yards with a marvellous economy of effort, combined with the gentle and precise touch of a surgeon. He achieves enormous leverage in the last foot before impact, which gives the impression that he is giving the ball a casual flick.

Only such an undemanding method could still look as majestic and functional as ever after such a time tramping the world's circuits. How fitting it was that de Vicenzo should add the one title he has coveted — since his first of ten attempts so narrowly failed at Muirfield in 1948 — to a list of over 30 victories in national championships. One can only wonder how many more he might have won had he possessed the same unswerving will to win that is the trademark of the "Big Three," or had he been able to putt only occasionally as well as any of that renowned trio.

Saturday was agony for me, so badly did I want to see the Argentinian win a championship in which he had finished second once and third no fewer than five times. Only last year, when he finished joint 20th, has de Vicenzo been out of the first dozen. But Player, Nicklaus, two and three shots behind respectively, so obviously meant business that I feared for this amiable, ambling giant from Buenos Aires. I had seen him blow his lead in the centenary Open of 1960 at St. Andrews, when he had started with two 67s to lead the field.

Everyone knew his temperamental weakness in a crisis. And when Player and Nicklaus sent out their caddies in advance to inspect the pin placings, and make a last check on their carefully plotted yardage charts, I must confess to having been convinced that the apparently casual manner of de Vicenzo would betray him in the face of such cold, mathematical expertise. How wrong I was to belittle natural talent. But I was not alone, even when de Vicenzo had only to play the last three holes, with the threat of going out of bounds at both the first two, and led Nicklaus by only three shots.

The crucial hole of the championship, however, was undoubtedly the dog-leg 10th. De Vicenzo had begun to look a trifle ragged at the 8th and 9th holes. Nicklaus was within two shots of him, as Player had remained at the turn, and there was now both the bulky American and the tiny South African to contend

Roberto de Vicenzo

with. I feared the worst.

De Vicenzo dispelled the doubts with a wonderful 9-iron shot that pulled up five feet from the hole. Player promptly three putted from nowhere across the steep slope, missing eventually from no more than a foot, and the Argentinian thus derived the inspiration to hole his putt. Thereafter the stunned South African faded quickly from the picture, and only Nicklaus remained as a serious threat. But when he failed to birdie the 14th his chance had virtually gone. De Vicenzo played a weak 4-iron to the 15th, recovered with a great bunker shot but never looked likely to hole out from five feet. He put the issue beyond doubt with the greatest golf shot I've ever seen — a towering 3-wood at the 16th across the out-of-bounds practice ground that exactly bisected the gap between the green-side bunkers. De Vicenzo's victory was a massive triumph of character in that he finally outsmarted the volatile temperament that had so long betrayed him.

(from *The Financial Times* Monday 17th July 1967)

SOME FURTHER IMPRESSIONS

We hope Ben Wright will forgive us here for allowing the words of Pat Ward Thomas's article in *Country Life* of July 20th 1967 to take Roberto down the final hole.

> The moment that will outlive all the others is of the last sunlit fairway, and Vicenzo, the look of an emperor about him, moving towards a reception which for sustained warmth and affection is unequalled in my memory. It was, after all, a sentimental occasion; the crowd had taken Vicenzo to their hearts, as everyone does who knows him. And how fitting of destiny to decree his triumph at Hoylake where, half a century before, Arnaud Massy had become the first champion golfer from a non-English speaking country. Vicenzo is the second; his place in history is assured.

Ben Wright's lasting memory of the Open was the scene before the final match went to the first tee. Gary Player "was sitting crosslegged on the edge of the putting green in silent meditation" whilst Roberto "on a bench beside the caddies shed, his tweed cap tilted back, his feet up was munching a sandwich and sipping a pint of milk". That is a far cry from the trifle that rounded off Harold Hilton's lunch seventy years earlier, prior to his final round in Hoylake's first Open Championship.

Mention of the sandwich reminds one of the article by Henry Longhurst in the *Sunday Times* describing the final day's play. The following words appeared — "The next vital moment came at the long 14th, where Nicklaus took the orthodox figure but Vicenzo pitched up with a sandwich, not only getting it dead but very nearly holding it..."

A letter some years later from a Hoylake member Philip Coard to Henry Longhurst brought the following reply.

> Dear Mr. Coard,
> Thank you so much for your cordial letter. I had forgotten the "sandwich" but remember it now. The sporting Sub-Editors never seemed to read the stuff at all and, after that, there came highly paid Readers, whose only job was to spot things like that — but they could not be ticked off because of the Union.
> I also remember Roberto's huge shot at the 16th. It seems a long time ago.
> Henry Longhurst

There are two other stories. Roberto had been staying with Roy Smith an ex-Captain of the Club, who in his early days with the Royal Insurance had spent some time in Argentina and had got to know him. Roy's near neighbours were the Rees Roberts, and Roberto had been entertained to drinks with them on a couple of occasions. Their young son David, aged 10 at the time, had chipped around the garden with the great man. On the day of the final round David had followed him all the way. At the last hole he had obtained a position right up beside the tee. Roberto spotted him as he was waiting to drive and said "Why do you no speak to me today David?"

The final touch was Roberto's invitation to Roy Smith to round up a few members to have a drink with him in the Club room after the prizegiving. About 25 members attended this delightful little party. He talked to everyone and even did a few tricks with ball and club. It was characteristic of the man that, in the hour of triumph, he could spend time with ordinary Club members. As he left, he slapped Roy on the back and said "How about that amigo? I just come back to see my friends and I win ze bloody Championship!"

LEADING SCORES

R. de Vicenzo	70	71	67	70	=	278
J. Nicklaus	71	69	71	69	=	280
C. Clark	70	73	69	72	=	284
Gary Player	72	71	67	74	=	284
A. Jacklin	73	69	73	70	=	285
H. Henning	74	70	71	71	=	286
S. Miguel	72	74	68	72	=	286
H.F. Boyle	74	74	71	68	=	287
T. Horton	74	74	69	70	=	287
P.W. Thomson	71	74	70	72	=	287
A. Balding	74	71	69	73	=	287
B. Devlin	70	70	72	75	=	287

'ALPS' (Tee)

The Amateurs

The Beginnings of the Amateur Championship

H.G. Hutchinson

Golf had jogged along very comfortably up to this time with its one championship, open to amateurs as to professionals, but never as yet won by an amateur. Then, in the winter of 1884–5 it occurred to some original genius of the Club at Hoylake — "why not a championship to be restricted to the amateurs?" I do not know whose great brain first flashed out the idea, but they wrote and explained it to me, asked me to serve on a Committee for the purpose, and gradually the scheme was licked into something more or less like shape. It was decided to hold, under the auspices of the Royal Liverpool Club, a tournament, under match play rules, open to all amateurs. The Club gave a handsome prize, or, rather, two prizes. I went up to Hoylake a little while before the affair came off, and there found the Committee in charge in something of a difficulty. Douglas Rolland had sent in his entry and they did not know how to deal with it. You see, at that date we had no definition of a professional, nor of an amateur, and had to decide on the analogy of other sports. I was all for accepting Rolland's entry then, and I am of the same opinion now — that it ought to have been received.

His offence was that, having come in second to Jack Simpson in the previous year for the open championship, he had accepted the second prize money, thereby violating the law common to several sports and pastimes forbidding an amateur to receive a money prize when in competition with professionals. That would have been all plain sailing but for the unfortunate fact that it was discovered that Johnny Ball, some years before, and while still quite a boy, had played himself into the prize list at an open championship and had been offered, and without a thought about the matter had accepted, a sum that I think amounted to no less than ten shillings. It was, of course, unthinkable that Johnny should be deprived of his birthright as an amateur for such a boyish error as this. There never was the faintest suspicion of professionalism

Horace Hutchinson, near the 1st tee

about any act of Johnny Ball's extraordinary golfing life, but technically, at that date, his case and Rolland's were very much on all fours. I saw that the Committee, or a majority of them, were resolved to reject Rolland's entry. I did not care to be a member of a Committee which rejected, for a cause I could not quite approve, the entry of one who would certainly be a very formidable competitor for a tournament which I had a distant hope that I might possibly win. I therefore asked leave to resign from the Committee, before the vote was taken on the point, and did so, with perfectly amiable sentiments all round. I have been rather long-winded perhaps in this explanation, but I wanted to make clear to those who are not informed about it the reason why the present amateur definition is drafted just as it is, with a time limit beyond which — that is to say before sixteen years of age — a man shall be held guiltless of having done any action to spoil his amateur status in playing for a money prize in competition with professionals.

So that was settled, and Rolland's entry disallowed. It passed off with less trouble than I had expected, perhaps just because Rolland was such a thoroughly good fellow, whether he were professional or amateur, and not at all of that small spirit which is apt to take offence where none is meant.

We set to work to play our tournament. It was considered best not to entitle it a championship, seeing that it was the installation of a single club only, and had no official recognition. Funny things began to happen from the start. It gave much delight to the men of Hoylake that I should have drawn, as my first foe, my old enemy at Westward Ho! Arthur Molesworth. Him I managed to beat with tolerable ease. I think he had even then begun to lose the sting of his game. After that I rather forget my fortunes until the semi-final heat, when I came up against Johnny Ball. In a previous heat, by the way, he had committed the crime of parricide, knocking out his own father, who put up a stout fight against him nevertheless. Johnny and I had a great contest, and I thought he was going to beat me, for he was two up at the turn; but I began to play rather well from there onwards and beat him by two upon the last green.

In that tournament we had not the arrangement which was made as soon as the amateur championship was put on an official footing — that is to say, in the very next year — of all byes being played off in the first round. The effect of that was that Allan Macfie, the other semi-finalist, had a bye in the morning. The final was decided in a single round to be played in the afternoon. I had been wound up to high concert pitch by that morning round with Johnny and could not play a bit in the afternoon. Macfie, on the other hand, putted like a demon and never made a mistake, so very likely the result would have been just the same if I too had been idle all the morning. He beat me, I think, by eight holes.

So that was the conclusion of it, and really it was most unfortunate for Macfie that he had not official right to place his name at the head of the list of amateur champions, for this was in all respects, except the title, equivalent to a championship. Leslie Balfour was not there, but Johnny Laidlay was. It was the first time that I made his acquaintance, though I did not have to play him. He was knocked out at an early period of the campaign. In fact I am pretty sure that he was not playing as fine a game then as he developed later. His putting, in particular, improved greatly, and so did the direction of his driving. His iron play was always, from the first, unsurpassed. I think that according to the arrangements of that tournament all ties must have gone on into the next round, for I well remember that Walter de Zoete tied twice with Macfie and was beaten by him on their third time of meeting, when Macfie, amongst other atrocities, did the short hole (the Rush Hole) in one. De Zoete went very strongly in the tournament. One of his victims was Mure Fergusson, whom he beat by eight and seven. There must, of course, have been something wrong here: I am not sure that gout would not come into the diagnosis.

And somewhere or other, among the crowd of lookers on at that tournament, with a heart very black with rage against me at my presumption in daring to beat the local hero, Johnny Ball, would have been a little boy of the name of Harold Hilton: a name to be heard of in later years.

That was the beginning, the preface, the preliminary canter, of the amateur championship, and it is to the initiative and enterprise of the men of Hoylake in getting up that tournament and conducting it to success, that we owe all the fun and all the tears we have had out of that championship since. No doubt it, or something like it, would have come sooner or later, whether or no, but it was due to the Hoylake Club that it came just as soon as it did. In the later course of that year it was taken properly in hand: the chief Clubs in the Kingdom gave it their sanction and subscribed to buy a challenge cup for it; rules were drawn up; the definition of an amateur was framed, and the first amateur championship meeting on these lines was put on the programme to be held at St. Andrews the following year.

(from *Fifty Years of Golf* published by Country Life Library 1919)

Editors Note: The suggestion that de Zoete and Macfie needed to play three rounds to settle the result is puzzling. The rule was that, in the event of a tie, both players moved forward to the next round. This indeed happened to Macfie in the first round, when he tied with W. Doleman. The handwritten results in the Royal Liverpool Minute Book show they played again in the second round. There is no such record of de Zoete and Macfie playing more than once either in the Minute Book or the press reports in *The Field* magazine.

The Amateur Championships (1887-1910)

Guy Farrar (with extracts from Horace Hutchinson, Harold Hilton and Bernard Darwin)

In the twenty five years following the 1885 tournament Hoylake were to stage the Amateur Championship on seven occasions.

1887

The competitors this year were the smallest in numbers, and the poorest in point of class that have ever entered for the event. All the great Scottish players failed to appear — it was said they felt it was useless trying to beat Mr. John Ball, Jun., on his own course.

Two interesting events were recorded — the entry of a very young golfer, almost a boy, whose name was Harold Hilton, and the fact that a father and son very nearly fought out the final together.

The semi-finals were played between Mr. John Ball, Sen., and Mr. Horace Hutchinson, and Mr. John Ball, Jun., and Mr. Jack Tait, an elder brother of the more famous "Freddy." The junior branch of the Ball family accomplished the task of getting into the final first — meanwhile his father was one up and two to play on Mr. Hutchinson.

Now let Horace Hutchinson take up the story:

So the conclusion of that nineteenth hole left me with John Ball, the elder, to play in the semi-final; and meanwhile that other John Ball, whom we distinguished as Johnny, was knocking Jack Tait out in the other semi-final. They were playing ahead of us, and as we went to the seventeenth (now the sixteenth) hole old John Ball was one up on me. And I had not played at all badly; only he had played in the most gallant way and had really hardly made a mistake. He was one up sheerly on the merits.

Then he said to me, as we walked after our second shots to the seventeenth hole and an emissary came back to say that Johnny had beaten Jack Tait, "It would be a funny thing if father and son had to play it off together." It was an innocent remark enough, and yet it nettled me a little, and I said in answer, "Wait a bit, Mr. Ball: you haven't done with me yet." Perhaps I ought not to have said it: it was rather a boastful answer. I can only plead the excuse of comparative youth. I sincerely hope it was not that reply which put him off his next stroke, but something bothered him as he played it. I saw him look up once, as he addressed the ball, at the legs of the people standing (or not standing as still as they should have been) opposite him. Anyone who knows Hoylake will know the stroke he had to play — to pop the ball over the cross bunker before the green, of the then seventeenth and now sixteenth hole. What happened was that he took his eye off and popped the ball into the bunker instead. I lofted mine over all right and won that hole. Then, by a lucky approach and a good putt, I got the last in three; and that was a stroke better than the hole ought to be done in and one too good for Mr. Ball.

So Horace Hutchinson faced up to the younger Ball in the Final, and Johnny failed to get revenge for the family, losing on the last green. The misfortune of breaking his brassie three holes from home contributed to the loss of his lead, and thus Hutchinson became Champion for the second year.

1890

In this championship the genius of Mr. John Ball, Jun., dominated the meeting. It was the third time the event had been held at Hoylake, and on the two previous occasions he had reached the semi-final and final rounds respectively. Now he was to record his first success on his own links in no uncertain manner.

Forty-four entries were received including all the leading players of those days, but everyone who crossed his path was treated the same way. Drawing a bye in the first round, he set out on his road to victory by beating Mr. Alex Stuart by six and four, a margin increased to eight and seven in the next round at the expense of Mr. James Fairclough.

Thus "the Champion-to-be" was brought face to face with a young Hoylake golfer of whom much was expected, Mr. H.H. Hilton. Mr. Ball finished the match on the sixteenth green, but in the middle of the round he was actually down to his young opponent. Coming events had cast their shadows before, and Harold Hilton had shown that he was a force to be reckoned with. Two years later these two were to meet in the final, with still the same result.

In the semi-final of 1890, Mr. Ball beat Mr. Leslie Balfour by six and five, and Mr. Laidlay beat Mr. David Leitch by one hole. The final was fought out once again by the heroes of England and Scotland respectively, and as in 1888, Mr. Ball emerged victorious. They had met at St. Andrews in 1889 in the semi-final and Mr. Laidlay had won on the nineteenth green after an historic match, but this year he was unable to check his opponent's triumphal career.

The final had to be postponed owing to a thunder-storm, and the wet greens suited Mr. Ball, who, by the aid of some brilliant putting, stood six up at the turn. "Never in the final of a Championship has a more brilliant start been made," is Mr. Hilton's description of the beginning of the round. The Scottish Amateur made a great fight coming home, but although he reduced the margin by two holes, the match ended on the fifteenth green, Mr. Ball winning the second of his Amateur Championship Medals.

As for the scores, Ball won by 4 and 3 and needed a 5 and two 4s for a round of 76 which would have equalled the record Medal score of the time.

1894

The final of this championship will always be remembered as one of the most exciting ever witnessed at Hoylake.

As in 1890, Mr. John Ball, Jun., treated all his opponents very severely, indeed on this occasion he was more relentless than usual and Mr. Laidlay, though beaten by five and three, accomplished the best performance against the "Hoylake terror."

The final looked to be going "according to plan," as Mr. Ball won the first four holes against Mr. Mure Fergusson.

One of the spectators was Harold Hilton, and his report continues:

... but he could get no "forrarder," and was surely and slowly pegged back. Holes kept disappearing with varying frequency until the whole four had vanished, with but two to play. There was naturally a good deal of excitement, and Scotland's representatives were wildly exuberant in their anticipations; and I remember one well-known Scottish golfer shouting out, "Johnnie Ball's beaten; he's funking." I didn't see him after the event, but it is more than probable that when he had seen the seventeenth hole played he had altered his key. There the gentleman who was presumed to be funking brought off a shot which will live in the memory of all who saw it. It was one of those strokes which will be handed down to history. Mure Fergusson had a fair drive; Johnnie Ball had a really good one, right down on to the old race-course. The former played very short with his second. Johnnie hesitated a moment, and then went for the green. He hit his ball as true as steel, and the ball in its flight hardly ever left the pin, and finished up just beyond the hole. It was a really *big* shot played at a trying moment, and just when it was wanted. He won that hole, and a half at the last hole sufficed.

Guy Farrar takes up the story again:

Sixty-four players took part, the largest entry ever received at Hoylake up to that time.

Mr. Hilton failed once again before his old enemy, Lieutenant Freddy Tait, being beaten on the last green after a game in which neither player did himself justice. He won the first two holes, but even this good start was of no avail. The malign influence that Freddy Tait exercised over Harold Hilton's golf was extraordinary, and only once has the Hoylake player been successful in their meetings.

Four Royal Liverpool players were included in the last eight — Mr. Ball, Mr. Hilton, Mr. Dick, and Mr. Macfie — but only one, the ultimate winner, reached the semi-finals.

1898

The idol of the Scottish crowds, Lieutenant Frederick Guthrie Tait, won this Championship, but in his journey to the final he narrowly escaped defeat on more than one occasion. In the third round he met Mr. Charles Hutchings, and the match ended all square. Playing the nineteenth he pulled his drive into the rough, but taking a wooden club, played a wonderful second to within a few yards of the hole. His opponent obligingly missed his third and lost the match.

Against Harold Hilton he won as usual with plenty to spare, and then had to meet the young Hoylake player, Mr. Jack Graham, Jun. The game depended on the holing of short putts and Jack Graham was found wanting, but if he could have holed-out with any confidence the winner of the 1898 championship would not have been Lieutenant Tait.

In the semi-final, having disposed of three of Hoylake's best players, he met Mr. John Lowe, and again nearly made his exit. Both were playing indifferently, but Freddy Tait saved himself again and again by his recovery shots. His drives mostly finished in the rough, but he generally managed to reach the green in the right number, and to hang on to an opponent who was playing the sounder golf. The match ended all square. The nineteenth was halved, but all seemed over at the twentieth where Freddy was left with a putt of seven yards for the half. With a despairing effort he holed it, and on the match went. At the Long he pulled out-of-bounds, and eventually put his fourth — a wooden club shot — within a few yards of the pin. His opponent who was on in three laid his fourth "dead," and again Freddy holed out. At the Cop, Mr. John Lowe failed on the green, and lost a match that has become famous.

In the final, the ultimate winner, playing much steadier golf, was too good for Mr. Mure Fergusson, and eventually won by seven and six. Lieutenant Tait was immensely popular at Hoylake, and his win was hailed with great delight.

Freddie Tait was remembered by the Hoylake members not just for his golf and his sportsmanship but for his high spirits. The strains of his bagpipes were heard in Market Street the evening before the Final and again in the Club room after his victory.

1902

With Johnny Ball back from the Boer War, Harold Hilton entering as the holder and Graham a semi-finalist in each of the two previous years, the locals must have felt confident of another home victory. It duly came, but from an unexpected quarter. It was Charles Hutchings, past Captain of the Club and, at the age of 53, a grandfather, who reached the Final. He proceeded to hole the course in 75 in the first round, an outstanding score at the time. After six holes in the afternoon he was 8 up, but as Guy Farrar recounts:

— surely a winning lead — but holes kept slipping away, some due to his own errors, others owing to those deadly pitch-and-run shots played by his opponent, Mr. Sidney Fry, until at the Dun his advantage had been reduced to two up with three to play.

He reached this green with two magnificent wooden club shots; Mr. Fry, who was short, played a good third over the cross bunker and holed out for a four, leaving the future champion, who had been very "lazy" with his approach putt, an awkward one for the half.

This was the crisis of the match. If he failed to hole this putt he would have lost seven out of the last ten holes — six out of ten was bad enough in all conscience. The putt dropped, and we breathed again! Mr. Fry, refusing to acknowledge defeat, won the seventeenth in four; but at the last hole his second was away on the right of the green, his opponent's ball lying about eight yards from the pin. Once again he played a beautiful run-up with his "jigger," leaving himself about four feet from the hole. Could the tired and weary Mr. Hutchings get down in two more? Eight yards can look a long way when, at the end of a championship final, two putts are required for victory. His first effort was a bad one — nothing like dead — but he holed the next amidst a mighty burst of cheering with which the Hoylake supporters relieved their pent-up feelings.

The "chairing" of Champions, carrying them shoulder high back to the Club house in triumph, had become the custom at Hoylake. In view of Hutchings' large lead at lunch time his supporters had carried the chair out to the far end of the course, waiting for the moment to lift their veteran hero. It and its bearers, becoming increasingly hot and embarrassed, followed from green to green, until their services were finally required a mere 200 yards from the Club house.

1906

Fourteen members of the Club out of a field of 166 entered but not one was to reach the last 8, the first time the Royal Liverpool suffered such ignominy.

"One of the poorest of all championships," was the general verdict on this Hoylake meeting. Some of the worst golf ever played in the last stage was witnessed in the final between Mr. Robb and Mr. Lingen. In the first nine holes of the afternoon round, when the famous half in nine occurred at the Briars, Mr. Robb — the ultimate winner — required 53, and his opponent 51 shots to reach the turn!

Mr. Robb won the first four holes in the morning round and eventually won the championship by this margin. The weather was bad — wind and rain — but the golf was worse, and this "umbrella" final was a poor ending to a championship meeting. It was "a Sunningdale year," as three members of that club figured in the last four.

Many favourites fell early in the struggle. Mr. Ball was beaten by his old opponent, Mr. Laidlay, who was afterwards defeated by Mr. Leathart — later a captain of the Royal Liverpool — then a member of Woking. Mr. Hilton, who was playing a poor game, was defeated by Mr. D. Ransom; and the reigning champion, Mr. Gordon Barry, was beaten by another Cambridge Blue, Mr. H.D. Gillies.

When the fifth round had been reached the prospects of Mr. Jack Graham, Jun. winning his first championship were very bright, as against Mr. Robb in the sixth round, he was two up at the turn. The match was square, however, at the end of the sixteenth hole, and Mr. Graham, playing a series of missed approach shots at the Royal followed this disaster by taking three putts on the last green —

1906 Amateur Championship
Top left: E.A. Smirke putting at the 11th green. Top right: C.C. Lingen at the 14th tee.
Bottom left: Robb bunkered at the 13th green. Bottom right: The morning crowd. Centre: James Robb, Champion.

so another chance of a championship medal went astray.

Before his victory at Hoylake Mr. Robb had twice been in the final and on two other occasions in the semi-final. He was a good golfer and a particularly beautiful putter.

1910

This championship in contrast to the one in 1906 was notable for the brilliance of the golf played. In the final Mr. John Ball gave an absolutely faultless exhibition, and the play of Mr. Jack Graham, Jun., until his meeting with Mr. Hilton in the sixth round, was a succession of wonderful outward scores. The golf all round was on a very high plane, scores of thirty-six for the first nine holes being quite common.

John Ball, 10th tee

Mr. Ball, then almost a veteran, recorded his seventh win, beating Mr. Aylmer in the final by ten up and eight to play. In the morning round his figures were:-

4, 4, 5, 3, 4, 5, 3, 5, 4 — 37
5, 3, 4, 3, 5, 5, 5, 4, 3 — 36 — 73

which included two stymies!

When the semi-finals were being played a Royal Liverpool final appeared a possibility, but as Mr. Aylmer was too good for Mr. Hilton, Hoylake was denied the spectacle of its two great players in opposition in the last stage. Mr. Abe

Far (8th) green looking north — Variety Club Tournament 1990

The 9th (Punchbowl) tee — Tim White (1990 Captain) driving

The Alps green — Easter Foursomes 1990

Hilbre (12th) hole — from the green looking east

Hilbre (12th) hole — from the green looking west

Crowds at the 14th green and 3rd hole

Views from the Clubroom

The Dee (10th) green from 11th tee

The Alps (11th) from the tee

Band of the Royal Marines at the 1983 Walker Cup Opening Ceremony

The Clubhouse

"Winter Foursomes — the Hilbre". Water colour by Ionicus

"Family Foursomes — the Far". Water colour by Ionicus

The Hall display

The Club Gold Medal

Mitchell, then playing as an amateur, reached the semi-final round only to fall a victim to the ultimate winner. Mr. Robert Harris in the preceding round had compelled Mr. Ball to obtain a three at the nineteenth hole before being finally disposed of, and in the fifth round Mr. Weaver was only beaten by the champion on the last green.

Before meeting Mr. Hilton, Mr. Jack Graham overwhelmed his opponents; playing Mr. H.D. Gillies he went out in 34 — his adversary, who had played perfect golf, being three down. Against Mr. Hilton his nerve gave way and the match became a procession.

In this championship occurred the historic scene at the nineteenth hole between Mr. Darwin and Mr. Horace Hutchinson.

Bernard Darwin tells the story:

Finally, though I hesitate to describe any game of my own in such good company, I did once take part — a very inglorious part — in an historic finish, and here it is to make a cheerful ending to the chapter. In 1910, at Hoylake, Mr. Horace Hutchinson and I met in the second round of the Championship. At the end of eighteen holes we were all square and went to the nineteenth. I had a moderate drive, he a good one well down to the left and clear of the corner. I played the odd and topped the ball hard into the turf wall which guards the out-of-bounds field, so that it fell back into the sandy ditch. Mr. Hutchinson, having about ten ways at his disposal of winning the hole, elected to try to lose it. He took a brassy and sliced out of bounds — the wind was blowing straight on his back. He dropped another ball and put that out too. At the third attempt he got well down the course, but not as far as the green. That was four. So far he had been the hero of the story. Now comes my turn. I ploughed my ball out of the ditch in three, and might with a really good cleek or spoon shot just reach the green. If I played safe I might hope for a half in seven, which would have been a direct gift from Providence. Being impiously greedy, being also no doubt in a state of some mental anxiety, I did not play safe, but went for the green with a driving mashie, and the wind blew the ball out of bounds. I had another shot with the driving mashie and the wind blew that ball out of bounds. I had a third shot with a precisely similar result.

Then having no more ammunition I gave up the battle. "And you two" said Mr. Angus Hambro as we walked in, "set up to teach people how to play golf!"

(excerpts from *The Royal Liverpool Golf Club* by Guy Farrar, *My Golfing Reminiscences* by Harold Hilton, *Fifty Years of Golf* by Horace Hutchinson and Bernard Darwin)

The Amateur Championships (1921 – 1975)

John Behrend

After the great war Hoylake's dominance of amateur golf was supposedly at an end. The American assault was about to begin, and the 1921 Amateur Championship was full of interest not least because they were here in force for the first International Match with Great Britain. Even so two members of the Club reached the last sixteen. One was John Ball, now in his sixtieth year, who after beating one member of the American team at the 19th in the morning succumbed to another, Frederick Wright, in the afternoon. Meanwhile Allan Graham, brother of Jack, having putted Bobby Jones out of his first Championship on a British links, beating him 6 and 5 in the fourth round, battled his way to the final. The sad news of his father's death during the night, and the play of William Hunter, very much the man in form, conspired to make the final very one-sided. Not even his caddie, none other than Campbell, could inspire him to stirring deeds. Hunter from Kent went on to play for Scotland, and then moved to California where he reached the semi-final of the US Amateur before turning professional in 1925.

In 1927 the home entry was numerically as great as ever. Of the seventeen members who had entered, the main interest centred on two — Harold Hilton and John Ball. In the words of Guy Farrar: "These two famous veterans were both trying to win their hundredth Championship round. They both failed, but in the moment of defeat, the years were lifted and we saw John Ball as in the days of old — he was dormy five down, but with a wonderful effort he obtained fours at the next two holes winning them both. We had visions of another great spurt but his opponent, Mr. Abercrombie, holed a long putt at the Dun for the match, and the old warrior went down fighting in his last game in the Amateur Championship." Froes Ellison, the English Champion, had been expected to do best of the Hoylake contingent but he had the mortification of knocking his opponent's ball into the hole when trying to negotiate a stymie from 5 feet at the 18th hole, thus converting probable victory into defeat. Eustace Landale, also from the home Club, reached the final against Dr. William Tweddell, but, like Allan Graham six years earlier, he could not do justice to the occasion. He won the first hole, but didn't win another one until he was nine down with nine to play. The winner was later to become Captain of the Royal and Ancient and an Honorary Life Member at Hoylake.

An unlikely record was established in the next Championship at Hoylake in 1933, when Michael Scott became the oldest winner. That Scott should win was no surprise, as before the 1914/18 war when he had lived in Australia he had won the Open Championship of that country twice and the Amateur Championship four times, but that he should win at the age of 53 on a course that had been lengthened especially for the occasion was certainly remarkable. About the length of the links Henry Longhurst was to write: "This was the beginning of an unhappy era in which we have successively lengthened the thirty odd thousand holes of golf in Britain to fit unsought 'improvements' in one ball instead of fitting one ball to thirty thousand holes; and Hoylake must have measured every inch of 7,000 yards. Not only that, but the walks to the far tees added fully a thousand yards of extra trudging — the tenth tee, for instance, being up in the sandhills, level with the place from which the players five minutes previously had played their second shots to the 9th. One is tempted, on contemplating this farcical development, due not to the wish of the ruling body but to the research departments of competitive ball manufacturers, to wonder whether, if the manufacturers of footballs discovered a ball, which when kicked from one end of the field would pitch at the other, every football club would rebuild its grandstands to accommodate the new ball!"

Scott, however, driving straight on the fast running fairways and holing more than his share of putts, with a putter borrowed for the occasion from his brother, won the semi-final against the much-fancied American, George Dunlap. 76 for the first round of the final was good enough to give him a 5 hole lead, and despite losing the first two holes after lunch he never allowed Dale Bourn, his popular young opponent, to get any closer, and he won at the 15th hole.

Hon. Michael Scott with trophy

In 1939 one name stood out in amateur golf. It was Jimmy Bruen, the long hitting Irishman with his much photographed loop. He was a strong favourite to win the Championship at Hoylake. On the way to a place in the quarter-final he had beaten John Graham. A crowd of 2,000 or so set off to see their local man, but the holes slipped quickly away and by the time the ninth tee had been reached, so John tells us, he was 7 down and they were playing by themselves. No one was there to see him pitch in for a 3 at that hole, and follow it with another 3, and then a 2 at the Alps to bring the margin of defeat down to respectability.

Bruen and Graham

Alex Kyle a Scot who played his golf in Yorkshire was Bruen's next opponent. Henry Longhurst later wrote: "A tremendous match it was with Kyle 1 up coming to the home hole. Here he laid the ball with a thump into the cross bunker in front of the green. With Bruen safely on in 2, a 19th hole seemed a certainty, and as Kyle descended to the bunker, the blue jerseyed stalwarts who man the rope were proceeding in advance to the first fairway. Their trouble was in vain, Kyle laid the ball stone dead and the match was over." Thereafter Kyle went on to reach the final and beat Tony Duncan from Wales. It was a well contested match — going to the 35th hole, but the most notable feature was the fact that they completed the first round in two hours twenty minutes.

It is not often in a match-play Championship that the two outstanding players in the field meet in the final. This certainly happened in 1953, the first occasion after the war that Hoylake staged the Championship. Harvie Ward, a US Walker Cup player, had won the previous year's Championship at Prestwick. Joe Carr, Ireland's leading amateur, was a match, not just for any other British amateur player, but for most of the professionals, but he had lost to Ward at Prestwick in the semi-final.

Apart from a tight match with Stranahan, Ward had proceeded to the final with a series of easy victories. Of his other opponents, the only one to take him as far as the 16th green was our own John Howard. Meantime Carr was struggling through with one victory on the last green and two wins at the 19th, including his semi-final match, where fellow Irish international Cecil Beamish obligingly put his second shot into the Field. That was the third time he had done it during the afternoon. His second shots at the 1st hole, and at the 16th, had suffered the same fate.

The players set off for the final with grey skies and a biting wind, such that Ward wore an overcoat between shots. Carr was 35 to the turn and 3 up, a lead which he still held at the end of the morning round. By the Alps in the afternoon he was back to all square, but Ward was bunkered from the tee at the next, and

Joe Carr driving at 17th (1953 final against Harvie Ward)

Carr took his chance there and he went 2 up with a 4 at the Field. Ward was not finished, and following a winning 4 at the Dun he played a long low iron shot on to the 35th green and it looked as though the match might well be squared again. Carr, however, thirty yards out, pitched near and holed. That was 1 up with one to play, and soon the new Champion was being borne aloft towards the Clubhouse on Irish shoulders.

Nine years later the Championship was back at Hoylake. Richard Davies, an American marine, unheralded as a golfer — though he subsequently played in the US Walker Cup team — won a close but somewhat scrappy final against John Povall the Welsh international.

"The most memorable battle," wrote Leslie Edwards, "was the one Brian Chapman, later to earn a Walker Cup place, and Joe Carr fought in a stiff wind of the kind which bares Hoylake's teeth. This ranks as the most remarkable match since the days when Ball and Hilton were pre-eminent. Chapman could do no wrong. It was as much as Carr could do to prevent his opponent going clean away. Chapman's shots to the greens were ruled on the flag. He putted brilliantly. When, at last, the match ended at the 17th green Carr, the loser, needed only a 4 at the last hole for a score of approximately 68. He said afterwards ... 'In all the matches I have ever lost it has always been possible to look back and see where I could have won. In this game I can't. However I had played I don't see how I could have beaten him.' John Graham and Roger Robinson, members of the Club, playing one couple ahead in the same round, spent so much time looking back to shots to greens they had just left, they lost sight of the certainty that their own figures would have won most of the ties played that day."

For the record Chapman went on to reach the semi-final where he lost by one hole to Povall, and Robinson beat Graham for a place in the fifth round.

1969 final finishes at the 16th

"This was in every sense a historic Championship, achieved in the centenary year of a Club which has played a bigger part in amateur golf than any other except the headquarters of the game." So wrote Peter Ryde in his review of the 1969 Championship for *The Times*. For the locals, apart from the encouragement of Michael Pearson working his way through to the quarter-final, the memory that will remain is of Michael Bonallack crouched low over his putter wrapping in putt after putt on the silky greens. In the final, time and again he holed the putts that break the spirit of an opponent, and that was just what they did to Bill Hyndman, who succumbed at the 34th hole. That, as Hoylake members know, is a very convenient place to finish, all the more so on that day, as the thoughts of many of the spectators were already turning to the dinner to be held that evening, presided over by Selwyn Lloyd, the Centenary Captain, with Gerald Micklem the R. & A. Captain, Willie Whitelaw and Joe Carr as the Guests of Honour.

Golf writers, as with racing correspondents, are not noted for their forecasting skills, but Peter Ryde ended his account of the final with the words "Such is one's faith in Bonallack that it is easy already to look forward to next year and the possibility that he might win for the third successive year, something which has never been achieved since the first Championship was held at Hoylake." That is exactly what he did achieve next year at Royal County Down.

1975 was a Walker Cup year and the Americans had won with a mighty strong side which included Curtis Strange, Jerry Pate, Craig Stadler, Jay Haas,

Gary Koch and George Burns. They all came to Hoylake for the Championship, and with Nick Faldo, Sandy Lyle and Mark James also playing, plus Nick Price and Gavin Levenson from overseas, readers could be excused for thinking that the writer had got confused and was describing a professional event of the following decade. The favourites fell thick and fast and only James and Price of those great names reached the last eight. James went on to the final where he played Vinny Giles, another member of the American team, but a combination of Giles' fine play and James' hay fever resulted in the American winning easily.

Once again a home Club player gave the locals something to cheer. It was Robin Biggs, a master at Birkenhead School, former Oxford Blue, and winner of the President's Putter. His chipping and putting were outstanding in beating Pat Mulcare, the Irish International, by 5 and 4 and then Gary Harvey for a place in the last eight. He lost next morning to Geoff Marks but doubtless can lay claim to the distinction of being the last player to compete in the quarter-finals of the Amateur Championship wearing a tie. Fashions change — one wonders who was the first to play without a tie.

The chapter closes with one personal memory of this Championship. The first day will be remembered for the gale force winds and the vicious rain and hail. One overseas competitor remarked that there were even white horses on the casual water. The writer, up against Willy Ferguson, a former Irish international, returned from the 18th hole cold, wet and dispirited after a last green defeat. He was greeted by a representative from the local press, who asked how he had done. Never at his most communicative after defeat, he referred the enquiry to the victor. That was a mistake, as in the press the next day appeared the following quotation from Willy Ferguson "It was nip and tuck for 14 holes, then I threw some 6s and 7s at him and that was good enough." That was not far from the truth, and this writer hasn't played in the Championship since!

The Matches against America— Previews

Bernard Darwin
and Donald Steel

In 1921, before the Amateur Championship commenced at Hoylake, an international match between the British and American amateurs was played. Bernard Darwin's preview of this match, to be the forerunner of the Walker Cup, was written with cautious optimism about the outcome.

The rain has flattered to deceive. We had a few showers and flurries of it yesterday evening and, once, it looked like settling in beneficently for the night, but it did not do so and today is a beautiful day with bright sky. The Welsh hills in the distance are looking less clear that they did yesterday. The wind, however, is whistling round the club house rejoicing in its strength. It is not a gale, but it is a fine Hoylake breeze, and another such day tomorrow should be ideal for the international match.

The British team that was chosen last night is much as anticipated. It seems a strong team now. What we think on Saturday night remains to be seen. It would be possible to choose another eight that would have quite as good a chance against it, but that is not the selectors' fault, but the result of the fact that there are fewer outstanding players than there used to be. Old age has been definitely "scrapped" in favour of youth this time. Nineteen years ago the first match between England and Scotland was played at Hoylake. A good many survivors of that remote geological era will be looking on tomorrow, but no one of the players of 1902 will be playing.

Youth is, of course, a comparative term. No one would accuse Mr. de Montmorency of "the atrocious crime of being a young man". He is the Nestor of the side, but is very fit and strong, with an ever youthful spirit and — which may be very important tomorrow — an experience of big matches and big crowds. Mr. Jenkins and Mr. Gordon Simpson are hardened veterans in experience, and Mr. Tolley, Mr. Wethered and Mr. Armour have crowded much big golf into a few years. It would have been pleasant of (*sic*) seeing Mr. Harris playing but he, I think, hardly "fancies himself" at golf just now. Better still it would have been to see Mr. John Ball and Mr. Hilton but, after all, youth will be served.

My own impression, for what it is worth, is that if our first three can do reasonably well we shall win, but they have their work cut out for them. We know little of the Americans as foursomes players; we think of them rather as four-ball match players. On our own side we have two couples from the Oxford & Cambridge G.S. who play many foursomes, and that should be an asset. But our best pair consists, I think, of the two Scotsmen, Mr. Jenkins and Mr. Simpson. Mr. Gordon Simpson is not, perhaps, very well known in the south, but no better testimony to his qualities can be given than in the words of a very great golfer yesterday — "I would rather see him playing the last hole before a big crowd than any other man in the field."

Mr. Chick Evans is said to be rheumatic today. He finished his yesterday's round limping perceptibly, and is resting. Mr. Bobby Jones too, went out in a thick sweater with a big collar and blew on his hands in the keen Hoylake wind. I suppose he is not used to this kind of weather, but I find it difficult to hope that it will affect him much. A swing so true and so easy, with such a perfect economy of body movement, can hardly do otherwise than accentuate its owner's merits in trying conditions. Mr. Hunter, who was playing with him, has a fine free swing too, but is something looser and less firm-footed, and he did not seem to relish the wind any more than most of us would do.

One experienced golfer said rather an interesting thing to me today, namely, that Americans today are playing rather as we did twenty-years ago — in this, that they trust more to a swing and a follow-through, whereas our players are trying to imitate the tremendous hit and snap of the professional. Like other interesting generalities this is not wholly true, but there is, I think, something of truth in it. Those who do not, like professionals, play golf every day, can have too much hit and too little swing.

Just as a post-script, I have seen Mr. Evans playing this afternoon, so his lameness is fortunately not serious.

(from *The Times* 20th May 1921)

Despite the home team's experience at foursomes play, the Americans won all four of the morning matches, and other than some splendid golf by Cyril Tolley who was out in 34 in the top match against Chick Evans there was little joy in the afternoon. The British team lost the match by three games to nine.

Twenty five defeats later (two victories and one halved game were all the British amateurs had to show for 60 years' endeavour) Donald Steel was previewing the 1983 match to be played at Hoylake. He wrote in more pragmatic terms:

The first requirement of previewers of the Walker Cup is a frank acknowledgement of the gulf that must exist between patriotism and realism. Every other year, optimism attempts to defy the inescapable fact of America's overwhelming supremacy.

Of the 28 matches played since 1922 Great Britain and Ireland have avoided defeat on only three occasions but, without the hope that this year might be different, all meaning would be lost from an event that has been productive of nothing but harmony and friendliness.

In a golfing world increasingly dominated by professionals, it is sentiment even more worthy of emphasis but, as both sides are launched on their preparations for this year's match at Hoylake on Wednesday and Thursday, the thoughts of both teams will be centred much more on the present. Awareness of tradition will be drawn later.

For the majority of the Americans the main problem will be the first acquaintance with a British course which, in the case of Hoylake, may not call for as much of the bounce and run that would be necessary in more normal Mays. As a result, they will be able to rely on hitting the ball up to the flag, a technique that comes naturally to them.

Their team is based on their victorious Eisenhower Trophy team of last autumn: Jay Sigel, Jim Holtgrieve, Bob Lewis and Nathaniel Crosby. But the strength of both teams may well lie in those new to international golf at this level.

Certainly we have learned not to base too much hope on the fact of an American team being largely unknown in this country and the British and Irish team will, if wise, not be guilty of unfamiliarity breeding contempt.

Whilst Philip Walton, Philip Parkin, Stephen Keppler, Malcolm Lewis and Martin Thompson will have learned great respect for the skill of so many young Americans, they will not be intimidated by them and, on top of that lies the claim that George Macgregor, Charlie Green, the captain, and David Marsh, chairman of selectors, had a lot to do with our last victory in 1971.

Add to that the experience of Arthur Pierse and the promise of Lindsay Mann, David Carrick and Andrew Oldcorn and there is no reason to be in the least downhearted, even if one or two are short of competitive practice.

(from the *Sunday Telegraph* 22nd May 1983)

The match, four foursomes and eight singles on each of the two days, was in the balance until the last hour. The teams were level at lunchtime on the second day and the British players started well in the singles. But the story on the scoreboard, which had a promising look to it as the matches went through the third hole, turned for the worse as the 5th, 6th and 7th holes took their toll. In the end the British could win only 2½ points in the final round of the singles, leaving the American team victorious again by 13½ to 10½.

The excitement of the match was not the only memory that will remain with Hoylake members. The flag raising ceremony in front of the Club house, the martial strains from the band of the Royal Marines floating over the first fairway, the large crowds of ardent amateur golf supporters, the friendship of our co-hosts from the Royal and Ancient and our visitors from the United States Golf Association, and from Philadelphia and California, and the cocktail parties and dinners all combined to demonstrate that, what had started at Hoylake 62 years earlier, was in good health.

The Ladies Championships — 1896 and 1989

John Graham and John Behrend

The fourth annual tournament for the Ladies Amateur Golf Championship took place at Hoylake from Tuesday 12th May to Friday 15th May 1896. It attracted more interest than ever before, not only among the ladies, but in the golfing community in general. For several days, prior to the Championship, open events associated with it were promoted by the West Lancashire Ladies Golf Club, the Moreton Ladies Golf Club and the Hoylake Ladies Golf Club (on what is now part of the Municipal Golf Course). Nearly all the Championship entrants competed at these preliminary gatherings, and were thus afforded an excellent opportunity of getting to know each other and seeing something of each other's golf. During the whole festival and the Championship the weather was fine and even oppressively hot. This resulted in very hard and fast fairways, and the greens were so keen that the competitors were put to a thorough test. Eighty-two ladies entered the Tournament, but four intimated that they would not compete. The main regret was the absence of Lady Margaret Scott, the holder and the only name then engraved on the Championship Cup, as she had won in each of the three previous years. She had decided, after winning in 1895, to retire from competitive golf. Another absentee was the famous Lottie Dod, five times Wimbledon Singles Tennis Champion. She had learnt her golf at Hoylake and would have been favourite to win. Unfortunately, she was enjoying herself in Switzerland at the time. The ordinary Medal course at Hoylake then measured 5,755 yards, but for this Championship it was reduced by over 1,000 yards to 4,730 yards.

In the early rounds, it is interesting to note that Miss K. Ball, sister of the famous John, managed to win her first two rounds. Another sister, Miss M. Ball, survived one round. Both sisters had entered from Moreton Ladies Golf Club. In

The competitors in 1896

The competitors in 1989

Miss Amy Pascoe

the semi-finals on the Friday morning there was a fair breeze. Three of the four players came from Wimbledon. In the first match Miss Pascoe played against Miss Moeller, from Ilkley. Miss Pascoe played the first six holes badly and was four down. She recovered extremely well and won the match by 3 and 2. The other semi-final between Miss Pearson and Miss Thomson was a give-and-take affair with Miss Thomson winning by one hole.

In the afternoon the wind dropped and the weather was fine and sunny. About 3,000 spectators appeared for the final to watch the two Wimbledon ladies battle for the title. Miss Pascoe won the second hole to be 1 up and was never headed. She eventually won by 3 and 2.

From Press reports at the time it is possible to obtain an accurate record of their scores at each hole, with the exception of the 9th hole. We do know that Miss Pascoe won this hole. In the figures below we have given her, perhaps generously, a 4 at the 9th.

Hole	*1*	*2*	*3*	*4*	*5*	*6*	*7*	*8*	*9*			*10*	*11*	*12*	*13*	*14*	*15*	*16*
Miss Pascoe	7	5	4	8	4	4	4	5	4	=	45	5	5	4	4	7	5	5
Miss Thomson	7	6	6	7	4	5	4	5	5	=	49	5	4	4	4	6	6	6

It must be remembered that all the ladies were playing with gutty balls and with hickory shafts, and that all of them, in the sultry hot weather, were wearing skirts down to their ankles and blouses fastened at the neck. They also wore boaters on their heads. It would not have been proper for them to have been otherwise dressed.

So to 1989. Things had changed — the standard of play, the mode of dress, the length of the course, the size of the crowds and the format of the Championship. Only the weather was the same. Warmth and sunshine (one thunderstorm apart) greeted the 95 competitors from eleven countries who played in the two rounds of stroke play to reduce the field to 32 for the match play stages. Sadly none of the five home Club players qualified. Unluckiest was Club champion Gillian Williams who had her problems on either side of the green at the Royal — bunker and Stanley Road — and holed out in 13.

Shorts were the order of the day, though slacks and even the odd skirt were also on display — the latter being a couple of feet shorter than those of the 1896 vintage. The course measured just over 6,000 yards, but with the fast running fairways most of the par 5s were in range in two shots for the younger and stronger competitors.

Helen Dobson from Lincolnshire aged 18, who was holder of the English

Ladies and English Girls Championship, reached the final against Elaine Farquharson, a 21-year-old Scot from Deeside. Saturday morning is not a time for attracting large crowds and there were only a few dozen there to see the opening drives, but the gallery had swelled to four or five hundred by the time the climax of the match was reached. Dobson's golf was near to perfection, but despite this Farquharson maintained her slow rhythm and was by no means outclassed or outhit. The English girl was 2 up on the 7th tee, and saw her opponent's iron shot come to rest some four feet from the hole. She followed it with an equally brilliant shot, and, putting first, holed for a 2. The Scot missed. Two more birdies followed and she had reached the turn in 32 to be 5 up. 4,3,4,3, from there was good enough to clinch the match by 6 and 5.

The most remarkable feature of Helen Dobson's performance was not however her play in the final, but the fact that she even reached the match play stages. A horrendous 8 (with two shots into the Field) at the very first hole in the first qualifying round led to an 81, which, though by no means a bad score, put her in danger of failing to qualify. When next morning she repeated the performance with two more out of bounds and another 8 at the 1st, and followed it with a 7 at the 3rd hole, the chances of reaching the match play stages looked distinctly fragile. With a true champion's character she played the rest of the round under par for a 76 and qualified with a stroke to spare.

There is one more fact to report, which says much for how amateur sport has changed in a hundred years. After the semi-finals the four competitors were summoned to the Ladies Changing Room ... for a drug test!

'ROYAL'

Some Hoylake Characters

Thomas Owen Potter

Horace Hutchinson

I fancy that all of us, speaking as golfers, had but one feeling when we read the advertisement of the Royal Liverpool Golf Club for a secretary, and that feeling one of regret that he who had held the post so long was about to leave it. It is perhaps, but a small matter that the duties for whose performance the club is now offering £200 a year were fulfilled by Mr. T.O. Potter for nothing. He was an honorary secretary; therefore, if the advertised rate represent the annual value of the services rendered, it is at once apparent how heavily the club is in his debt. Yet this is not a true statement, or is, at least, not the whole truth; for not only did Mr. Potter give to his work a loving labour which money cannot buy, but he also helped, in very large measure, to bring the club into its present position and affluence, which make the secretarial duties so arduous and worthy of such a recompense. He was, in fact, the creator of duties which another will only have to carry on along the lines which he has laid down for them.

Thomas Owen Potter

Perhaps any man can give attention to duties of this nature, and every man, according to his lights, can show courtesy in their fulfilment; but to these talents Mr. Potter added one which no effort can simulate — a true gift of the gods, which flows unstrained as the quality of mercy from those who have it — the great, the invaluable gift of geniality. To meet his hearty welcome after the harassing complication of train and tram and steamer, by which in old days one arrived at Hoylake, was like coming into sunshine weather after an April shower. His kindly sympathy when a match was over robbed defeat of half its bitterness, and the victor felt his victory but incomplete until it had been told at length to the much-enduring secretary.

Tom Potter — I really cannot go on calling him "Mr." — was honorary secretary for the better part of twenty years; and that is a big slice of his life for a man to devote to unpaid work in the service of his fellow creatures, even when they are fellow-golfers. He saw the club rise up to its present importance out of the initial efforts of some few Scotsmen, resident in Liverpool, who came down to contest possession of the links with the rabbits. At first the course used to be all rabbit-holes and racecourse posts. Now one never gets into a rabbit hole, unless one is off the course; and if a solitary racecourse post yet remains, it ought to be silver-mounted and presented to Mr. Potter, with a golfer, or a rabbit, or some such hole-boring vermin, on top of it, to remind him of days of which no one can have a clearer memory than he. It is not the first baton which has been given him in grateful recognition of service rendered. Who that went to Hoylake in the old days has not a lively recollection of the musical evenings in the bar parlour, when Potter himself did the lion's share — a lion of most melodious roar — of the singing, or when he conducted the chorus to Mr. "Pendulum" Brown's famous rendering of the "Farmer's Boy," or an operetta composed to do honour, by "topical" references, to the stirring doings of the week? His "Hech, diddledee, and the Lowlands Low!" used to be given with a *verve* that aroused enthusiasm such as the written words of that quaint refrain do not seem to suggest at all. It was by his way of rendering them that they were made to seem so great, and it was in virtue of his conductorship on these and like occasions that Mr. Potter was presented with the baton which he wields so successfully at the Golf dinners at Hoylake to-day. His voice, if I do not mistake, was well known on tours of the Free Foresters' Cricket Club before the good fortune of the Royal Liverpool Golf Club turned his attention to Golf.

As a golfer he played just exactly the sort of game that an honorary secretary ought to play. He was never in the first rank — you do not want a champion player for your secretary; he would be apt to think more of Championships than of the club business — but he played well enough to give a good match and a beating to the great majority of strangers who turned up at a loose end for a game. The good match and the good company made them think that everything was pleasant, and the beating kept them humble as a stranger ought to be. Mr. Potter was always ready to play with any of these forlorn ones. Once the present writer tied with the honorary secretary for the handicap prizes. The first prize was a salad bowl and ladles, the second a butter dish — articles which combined the *utile* with the *dulce,* as a reward of merit. As the result of playing off the tie, the salad bowl fell to the writer, and the honorary secretary had to find his consolation in the butter dish. But, as if to show that she recognised the inadequate recognition of the secretary, Fortune decreed, for the salad bowl, another fall — off the porters truck on the Hoylake railway platform, whereby nothing of value was left of the salad bowl except the silver rim, which may be worn as a halo, and the spoon and fork.

After mention of these truly great qualities of Mr. Potter as a secretary, it seems a small thing to say that he performed to perfection the minor but infinitely laborious business of the club, arranging its meetings, ordering its finances, and the innumerable details which required daily attention. Had it not been for his unnoticed share in the work, it is possible that Hoylake might not have had the honour of inaugurating the Amateur Championship competition which at once received general recognition and became an annual fixture. At all the big meetings of which Hoylake is now the arena Tom Potter is always present to work the machinery with his unremitting attention, and to lubricate its wheels with his unfailing courtesy.

With all this, and after so many years of office as a permanent official, he has never, I fancy, been known to arrogate to himself even that share in the direction of matters connected with the club to which his long experience might have reasonably entitled him. Rather he has seemed to show what might have been deemed an excess of modesty in listening to, and requesting suggestions from, any who were disposed to offer them, and with most devoted and unselfish loyalty has shown care for nothing but the best interest of the club. A tolerably long and extensive acquaintance with members of the Royal Liverpool Golf Club has not revealed to the writer one single enemy of Mr. Potter, and it is very doubtful indeed if any other man has ever held such a post so long and left it with such a record. Of the friends that he has made in that capacity, the list is probably to be read in the lists of those who are now, or ever have been, in any way connected with the club.

Enough has been said to show how very difficult will be the task of him who has to fill Mr. Potter's place. Neither £200 a year, nor so many thousands, can be expected to purchase one who shall combine, so ideally well, the qualities of a secretary. Yet we may hope that for many years the atmosphere of the Hoylake meetings will be gladdened by the presence of Mr. Potter's geniality, and the choruses conducted by his practised baton. What the club will do without his services one cannot think nor yet what Mr. Potter will do without his duties.

(from *Golf* August 10th 1894)

Allan Macfie

John Graham

Allan Macfie was born on 8th February 1854 and died in 1943. He married Isabel Tarbet in 1878. He was educated at Edinburgh Academy but, in spite of the proximity of the North Berwick and Bruntsfield Links, he seemed to have no inclination to play golf. He started to take an interest in the game in his early twenties and it was not until he came to Merseyside in 1879 that he really took the game seriously. He was rather small and slim and he was stone deaf. In his case this was literally true, as he had been thrown a year or two earlier in Australia by his horse into a heap of stones which resulted in complete incapacity of hearing. He learned very quickly to lip read, but unless he was facing a person, he could not know what was being said. When he was playing in the Final against Horace Hutchinson in the first Championship a spectator went up to his side and congratulated him on a marvellous shot he had played. When Allan Macfie did not reply, he repeated his congratulations — still with no response. The spectator moved back into the crowd muttering "what a surly brute". He did not know he was stone deaf.

He was exceedingly thorough in everything he did. According to the golfing scribe, H.S.C. Everard, he was "precise with an unwonted precision. He was always to be relied upon to a moment for an engagement, especially a golfing one; he always knows what train he is going by, and never misses it; he is always provided with a pencil in his pocket and a knife to sharpen it with, and a paper whereon to write; and if he is playing whist he never fails to have his honours marked, if entitled to them, the very instant the hand is over."

A real "so and so" to be avoided at all costs, it might be thought. But not at all. He was popular. He could at a moment's notice do conjuring tricks. He was always full of anecdotes and conundrums and would recite witty little rhymes which were so much the vogue of the time. I am sure that the following puzzle, which was going the rounds at the turn of the century, would have been a favourite of his. It was a poem with three missing words. Each word was of eight letters and was an anagram of each other.

"Off to the Links is now the cry,
For Golf is man's ....
Be not ...., be not slow,
.... hit, the ball will go."[1]

He was also a first-class photographer and he took pictures wherever he went as he travelled a great deal. His albums were in great demand by his friends. But his pride and joy was his workshop in which he spent many happy hours designing and making his own clubs and numerous experimental ones, as he was a great theorist. He made his own fishing rods and even his own pipes.

He is best known for his golf and the fact that he won the first Amateur Championship in 1885. His preciseness, his attention to detail, his determination to do well and the litheness of his body, all ensured that he would be a top golfer. He had very supple hands and wrists. He was a very dedicated golfer who studied every move of the game with almost scientific attention, and was the first great practiser. Harold Hilton became a disciple of his and practised a great deal. Allan was not a long hitter, but because of continual practice, and a perfect mechanical swing, he was seldom in real trouble and was a very, very good putter. According to one acquaintance "He could putt with anything, from a fire-shovel to a Philp." He began to win medals in 1880. Soon after winning the Amateur in 1885 he left Hoylake for St.Andrews and it was not long before he was winning there and at Carnoustie.

How he won the first Amateur has been chronicled elsewhere. It was an odd Championship. If two contestants halved their match, then both went through to the next round and continued the battle there. This is exactly what happened to Allan Macfie, who halved his first round with W. Doleman but beat him in the second round by 5 and 4. In the fourth round he had a hard scrap with W.M. de Zoete and only won on the last green, having holed The Rushes in one, needless to say the first to be recorded in an Amateur Championship. A new draw was made for each round with the exception of those who had halved in the previous round. This eventually resulted in three contestants reaching the last stages instead of the normal four. Consequently one of the last three had a bye into the final and this lucky golfer was the ultimate winner, Allan Macfie, who defeated Horace Hutchinson by 7 and 6.

The Macfies and the Grahams were related and I called in to see him at St.Andrews just before the last war. I found him a little bent, stone deaf (he reprimanded me for shouting at him), but still a man of immense spirit.

[1] The answer to the word puzzle is — idolatry, dilatory, adroitly

John Ball

Bernard Darwin

A man I knew, finding himself sitting at Lord's next to an old gentleman of venerable aspect, asked him if he had ever seen Alfred Mynn. "Sir", said the old gentleman, "I bowled him out". I suppose that those who knew and played with John Ball are now almost coming to that stage. Let me try to say something about that truly historic figure, beyond question the greatest amateur golfer that this country has produced.

It is twenty years since he died. There was always some little mystery as to his age, but the book says he was born in 1861. He won eight Amateur Championships and one "Open" and was sixth in the "Open" when he was fifteen years old. The sixth prize was ten shillings, which as any reasonable schoolboy would, he put in his pocket.

When, some years later, an amateur had to be defined for championship purposes, the age at which it was permissible to have won a money prize had to be settled accordingly; otherwise the purest and most genuine of all amateurs might have been disqualified — an odd little piece of history.

In one sense I regard John Ball as the greatest of all golfing heroes, judged by the overwhelming hero-worship that he inspired at Hoylake. It came to him all uninvited for he was by nature a modest, reserved and silent man. Yet you could not go to Hoylake without hearing of some shot he had played or something that he had said. When he was engaged in a great match there, all the world waited for news of him.

I always think of him setting out with a rose in his buttonhole, and his stockings with red tops, guarded by a band of fishermen holding the rope. It was a memorable and somehow an oddly touching sight. The very errand boys on the road neglected their work and leaned on their bicycles to watch prayerfully the great man. He repaid this adoration with no ostensible gratitude, and the story was told of how, when he was coming home after some victory, and there was to be a great reception for him, he got out at the station before Hoylake and walked back across the links all unseen.

Hoylake was his home where he was born. His father and grandfather before him owned the Royal Hotel which looked out on the Royal (or 17th) green, once upon a time the first. The clubrooms were built on to the hotel and there were famous meetings there in early days when leading amateurs came down from Scotland to play in these meetings, bringing their henchmen, Jamie Anderson and Tommy Morris with them. It was told of Jamie Anderson that, defeated by the narrow shot to the present first hole, he exclaimed, "Ma God, it's like playing up a spout".

John Ball (left) talking to Harry Vardon (right) at 1936 Open

At those evening meetings there was frequently heard the

voice of John's father, a sturdy and resolute golfer who made himself somehow into a rather good one, "Me and my son will play any two". And the gauntlet was not often picked up.

I could lose myself for ever in these legends of old Hoylake, but must come back to John as a player. He was a great and fascinating one with, to my mind, the most perfectly rhythmical swing conceivable. The underhand grip of the right hand was not pretty, but it was far more delicate than it looked, and the swing was, to use an old cliché, the very poetry of motion.

I believe when he was young, he played with the ball far back opposite his right foot which enabled him to hit great carrying shots up to the pin to drop dead there; but when I knew him that had become too hard work for his back and he had a more normal stance.

However he stood he was abnormally straight. Harold Hilton always told me that it was John who first showed the world how the ball could be hit straight up to the green with wooden clubs; an art with which J.H. Taylor, another great and accurate driver, has been credited.

He was a grand iron player and had, with iron clubs, a peculiar gift of being able to get the ball high and straight into the air with a straight-faced club. He would play his pitches with an iron rather than with a mashie, and I believe the only championship final he ever lost was at the 19th hole at St. Andrews against Leslie Balfour-Melville when he took the unaccustomed mashie to pitch over the burn and pitched plump into it.

He was, I should say, a resolute putter in the sense of attacking the hole, as people say nowadays, and I can think of one or two very good ones that he holed at supremely critical moments, but I would not call him, on the whole, a good putter; a good approach putter perhaps, but rather shaky over the short ones now and again. It was his weak spot, the only one he had. He was a great finisher and a fierce pursuer, who rather enjoyed a stern chase than otherwise.

As an example of one of his rather odd characteristic remarks, Lord Wardington told me how, in his very first championship, when he was at Oxford, he drew John Ball at Hoylake and started off gloriously by winning the first four holes. Then the giant woke and bestirred himself, the holes came back very quickly, and young Mr. Pease, as he was then, was beaten some way from home.

On saying the right thing to his conqueror, he received the reply, "I thought we were going to have a good game". It was, I believe, an entirely sincere answer. His notion of a good game was to be some holes down and then to get them back. "Now watch John save his half-crown", people used to say of some friendly game in which he was one down going to the home hole. He had a knack in such circumstances of doing it in 3.

Alas, I did not see John win the "Open" at Prestwick in 1890 as it was a little too early for me, though I well remember the excitement. It was, as Dr. Laidlaw Purves said, "A great day for golf. The first amateur and the first Englishman!" I watched three of his victorious finals, at Prestwick in 1899, at Hoylake in 1910 and at Westward Ho! in 1912.

It was perhaps in the Hoylake match that he played the most perfect golf, for he beat a very good golfer, C.C. Aylmer by 10 and 9. W.B. Stoddart, great rugby football player and cricketer, was captain of the Royal Liverpool Club that year and John had said to him, "Wilfred, I should like to get a medal from you", and proceeded to do it.

It was the other two matches that were the most dramatic, especially that at Westward Ho! where there was a wind blowing, and it was then that John was most exciting to watch. In 1899 at Prestwick his opponent was Freddie Tait, and at one time it seemed that the Scotsman would run away, for he was five up at the 14th in the first round. Then he seemed to relax a little (he said afterwards that he had learned a lesson in that respect), and was pulled down to three at lunch.

After lunch everyone watched John Ball on the last green having a putting lesson from Hilton, for he had been missing some easy ones in the morning, and now he tried all possible clubs, a swan-necked putter, a driving cleek and even an iron, not for the moment with any noticeable success, but he improved when the game began again.

That last round has been described very often, how John squared the match with six to play and was one up going to the 17th where Tait played an historic shot out of water in the Alps bunker and John followed it with one equally good off the hard wet sand close to the sleepers; how Tait halved the match with a most gallant 3 at the home hole and John countered it with a glorious 3 at the 37th, when he really did hole a putt. The Hoylake supporters did not see it. They had hidden themselves in the club house, unable to bear it.

At Westward Ho! he had an equally great finish against Abe Mitchell, at that time an amateur from the Cantelupe Club, Forest Row. What a match that was! With Abe hitting tremendous distances and gaining a lot in length, he was three up at lunch but John told his friends that if he could halve the first three holes where Mitchell would have the better of him in the wind for length, he thought he might just do it. He went one better for he won one of those first three holes and soon he had squared the match.

Then came a terrific tussle. At all square with two to play, John made a shot very unlike him for he put his second in the big cross-bunker and Mitchell won it comfortably. Then Mitchell ought to have settled it at the 18th, but he missed a putt of four or five feet for the match (I can still see his despairing gesture), and John rammed his putt of about the same length straight home. The 37th was halved, but at the 38th poor Abe topped his tee shot into a ditch straight in front of his nose, and that was the end.

John sometimes made prophetic remarks. Harold Janion, the secretary of Royal Liverpool, had said to him, "The last time I watched you I had to go to the 37th." John answered, "This time you'll have to go to the 38th."

It was the only match in which I ever saw politics play a most unwelcome part. The members of some sort of radical club out of Bideford came out to support the working man in the shape of Abe Mitchell against the aristocrat, singularly enough represented by John Ball. Their behaviour was venomous and offensive and they did no good to their own man for Abe was far too good a sportsman to be anything but disgusted. As to John, if it had any effect on him, and none was visible, it made him set his teeth harder than ever.

That was John's last victory. He intended to defend his title at St. Andrews in the following year and set out on his motor cycle, a recent acquisition, but something went amiss and he never got there. He played again at Hoylake when the Americans invaded us in full strength, but did not survive to the end. It was hot, calm weather and he wanted rain and wind. Then he would have been in his element.

He left Hoylake after his marriage and went to live on a farm in Wales but came to his old home now and again on big occasions. A young friend of mine who was acting as a steward was shocked to the core. "I've nearly done such an awful thing", he said. "I saw an old gentleman where I thought he ought not to be. I was just going to shoo him away when I saw it was John Ball." That would have been awful indeed.

(from *Golf Monthly* August 1960)

Harold Horsfall Hilton

John Turner

It seems appropriate that Harold Hilton's arrival on this planet should have coincided with the formation of the Royal Liverpool Golf Club in 1869. Over Hoylake's links he learnt his golf and was soon to contribute in good measure to the lustre of the Club by splendid achievements not only there but elsewhere in Britain and eventually in the United States.

He has recorded some of his very early golfing ambitions. At the age of seven, with a few other young enthusiasts, he liked to attempt to drive a ball over the bowling green of the Green Lodge Hotel in Hoylake. This they passed each morning on their way to school. The carry involved was some 30 yards and there was a prominent notice indicating that trespassers would be prosecuted, which meant that a failed effort would have to be retrieved after dark. For the young sportsmen proceeding on their way, there followed another challenge, involving a carry over the garden of one Mr. Wilson, known locally as the "Chieftain". This gentleman had caused to be displayed a large notice saying "Beware of the Dog". The competitors, albeit of tender years, soon appreciated that whereas the prosecution of a trespasser might be cause for concern some time in the future, the dog would be interested only in the present. Although the garden was no wider than the bowling green, to negotiate it satisfactorily was regarded as the greater achievement in view of the consequence of failure — early awareness of the influence of psychology in the game of golf.

At the age of seven or eight he used to borrow one of his father's hats so as to look a seasoned golfer. The hat, far too large, invariably flew off young Harold's head before the finish of the stroke. This impish sense of fun apparently stayed with him through the years and by virtue of his fast swing and whirlwind follow-through, his cap, perched usually to the back of his head, continued to fall to the ground from time to time.

He had a natural aptitude for a number of sports and when away at school he excelled at cricket, football, fives, swimming and sprinting, and as a boy he won a number of medals at Hoylake for sons of members. By his seventeenth year there can be no doubt that golf had become his favourite. On leaving school he had a long summer holiday while his parents were considering his future career. Happily he found a number of good advisers, who spotted his natural talent. William More, a few years Hilton's senior, was a skilful and knowledgeable golfer, who would probably have made a considerable impact himself had his health not been suspect. Hilton has recorded the great debt he owed to More in the development of his game. He also had the good fortune to be befriended by John Ball, already established as one of the finest players in the land. As the years passed, the two were to feature together in contests of the highest order.

Short in stature, about 5 foot 7 inches, but powerfully built, Hilton developed a sound technique. He could draw or fade as required and was a master of back spin. His pitch and run with his mashie became deadly and he putted well, rolling the ball with top spin. He acquired a reputation as a cheerful character, but definitely a man to be reckoned with. One who played with him during his great days has described how he relished the big occasion, the meetings with many friends, the excitement of a championship and the dust of battle.

In the early stages of his career some shrewd judges of his game declared him to be better by about two shots per round when playing to a card than in match play. This may have been true initially, and it is interesting to note that he won his first Open at the age of twenty-three in 1892, his second Open in 1897 but had to wait until 1900 for his first Amateur Championship. Prior to winning the Amateur he had been runner-up on two occasions, and had defeated many distinguished golfers on the way. His final tally of two Open Championships, four Amateur Championships and the U.S. Amateur gives him a place among the golfing giants.

Hilton's first Open win was extraordinary in many ways. To start with he very nearly did not get there. The previous year he had played in his first Open at St. Andrews and finished equal eighth. In 1892 at Muirfield the Open was for the first time played over four rounds, two per day, on Wednesday and Thursday. Parental wishes were apparently against his participation on the grounds of expense and his father's poor opinion of the new Muirfield course. But Hilton received an invitation to stay with a friend in Gullane and with this in his favour he was given a belated go-ahead on the Monday of the Championship week. He caught the night train from Liverpool and arrived in Gullane for breakfast on Tuesday. That day he played three practice rounds in preparation for the following two days. The field included many distinguished amateurs including his friend John Ball but by this time the main golfing talent was in the professional ranks.

Hilton's rounds of 78, 81, 72 and 74 were regarded as a tremendous achievement at that time. In his own opinion his first round was "fairly good". It left him four shots off the lead. His second round was almost a disaster. He took 36 shots to cover the first seven holes and thought he was out of contention, but some side bets with two friends made him determined to save his stake if he could. He reached the turn in 45, then came home in a splendid 36, which left him eight shots behind the leader.

The nightmare of the previous afternoon turned into a golfer's dream on Thursday morning — out in 35 and rock steady coming home for a splendid 72. This put him in second place, two shots off the lead. His 74 in the afternoon contained a number of adventures, but his splendid short game stood up to the pressure throughout, especially his pitch and run with his mashie. He holed twice from twenty yards or more. He was out late in the field, and knew what he had to do as news of his rivals came back to him. He was able to indulge in a 6 at the eighteenth and still win by three shots from the trio who tied for second place — Hugh Kirkaldy (winner the previous year), Alex Herd and John Ball.

For a few years after that he performed creditably in many major events, including the Open, but still the feeling existed that his win at Muirfield was a freak result. 1897, with the Open at Hoylake for the first time, was to disprove that. The story of that victory has already been told; he won with Vardon, Taylor, Braid and Herd all in the field and his final round of 75 was a triumph of technique and temperament.

After his second Open victory Hilton's friends suggested he might now address himself seriously to the matter of becoming Amateur Champion. It was three years later he achieved this at Sandwich. That year, 1900, there were two notable absentees. Freddie Tait, soldier and sportsman, had become one of the most exciting amateur golfers in the short span of life allowed him. Hilton admired and liked Tait but admitted he was the one he most feared in competition, with good reason for Tait was victorious in all their major encounters. John Ball was away too on active service in South Africa. Hilton met his clubmate, John Graham, in the semi-final on a day when everything went Hilton's way. He started by holing a full second shot at the 1st. In the final against James Robb he was 3 up at lunch and won by 8 and 7.

At last he was Amateur Champion and he followed this by winning again next year at St. Andrews. In an exciting and up-and-down final he beat an old friend John Low of the R & A on the last green, and received generous applause from a gallery understandably partisan in Low's favour.

Other interests took much of Hilton's time for the next few years but he re-entered the fray in 1910 and reached the semi-final of the Amateur at Hoylake. Then in 1911 he won the title again, this time at Prestwick. In a strong field he played brilliantly and did not have to go beyond the 13th until the sixth round. In the final he beat E.A. Lassen of Lytham St. Annes. He followed this by a fine performance in the Open at Sandwich, when he finished one shot behind Vardon and Massy, who tied for first place.

He then set off for the 1911 U.S. Amateur Championship at Apawamis Links. He made a fine start by winning the Medal for the best qualifying score. After some notable scalps he reached the final to play Fred Herreshoff, who had beaten the much fancied Chick Evans in the semi-final. Hilton was 4 up at the half way stage but Herreshoff was a great fighter and not only got back on terms but was 1 up after thirty holes. In a tense contest of nerve and skill Hilton came back to win at the 37th hole. So in what must have been the greatest year in his golfing life, he held the two Amateur Championships and was one shot adrift in the Open.

Back home he won the Amateur again in 1913. He came through a field of fine golfers to win the final by 6 and 5 against Robert Harris, who survived to win the Amateur in the 1920s and to play in the Walker Cup.

This really was the finale. In 1914 the clouds of war blotted out the golfing scene and Britain was locked in mortal combat for over four years. Hilton did play in some of the Championships of the 1920s but without conspicuous success. The scene had changed; much of the old blood sadly was missing and the years had taken their toll.

His proud record remains for all to see.

Charles Hutchings

Roger Robinson

Hutchings was born in 1848 at Thorverton, North Devon, where he spent his early childhood before being educated at King William's, Isle of Man. He was married in 1873 to Marion Somervail Balfour of Edinburgh and had two sons and three surviving daughters. It is uncertain when he moved North, but by his early twenties he had inherited all or part of a tannery in Warrington. According to his grandson, John Hutchings, he retired at the age of 27 but retained several non-executive directorships. As will be mentioned, he was a fine all-round sportsman and, apparently, somewhat despised the game of golf originally, preferring other sporting pursuits. He was introduced to golf by John Dun who hailed from Warrington, and was the third Captain of Royal Liverpool and an original member, after whom the 16th hole was named. A doughty player, he taught Hutchings, then aged 30, and evidently fired him with great enthusiasm for the game.

From the records of the Club and of the Amateur Championship, it is amply evident that from 1885 Hutchings had arrived as a power in the golfing land and at Hoylake in particular. Though he is shown, on occasions, as entering from Frodsham and also Warrington, he was by now living in Hoylake, where he stayed until 1906. It is equally clear that Hutchings was a pillar of the Club. As well as being one of its leading golfers he was Captain in 1890. He won many Club events such as the Dun Challenge Cup (three times), losing a fourth in 1900 in a play-off with Harold Hilton, the Lord Stanley of Alderley's Medal, the Hall Blyth

Gold Medal and the Kennard Medal. For the twenty years 1885–1905 he consistently played for the Club team at number four, and when you consider that he was preceded by John Ball, Harold Hilton and Jack Graham Jr. this is the measure of his stature as a Hoylake golfer.

As was customary for a leading player, he travelled extensively to compete and he made his mark at the Royal and Ancient Golf Club of St. Andrews by winning the Jubilee Vase in 1894, the Silver Cross in 1896 and the Bombay Medal in 1900. He won too at Formby and Royal Lytham.

Hutchings had a style all of his own, a little stiff and short by standards of the time, but it worked for him. Despite the technical impurities or even heresies in his swing, Hutchings drove a fine long low ball with slight draw, played his irons strongly, usually with a bit of fade so that they dropped and did not run, and had the dexterity around the greens of a fine billiards player. He must have been possessed of considerable physical strength to play the game as he did — especially in the wrists and arms.

We have noted Hutchings' development and success in the highest golfing circles from 1881 and by the turn of the century — he was 52 in 1900 — it could reasonably be supposed that he would decline as a force in the game. He had played in representative matches, few though there were in this era. For example, he played at Sandwich in 1894 for the Amateurs against the Professionals.

He was moderately successful in the Amateur up to 1900 losing in the third round, and otherwise usually in the second. However, as he was twice beaten by Harold Hilton, twice by Freddie Tait and once by Allan Macfie, he was not disgraced. In 1901 at St. Andrews he was beaten by one hole by Horace Hutchinson in the sixth round, which was a sterling performance. Though he could hardly have known it at the time this was an augury for the events of the following year.

1902 was a momentous year for Hutchings. The powers that be at Hoylake had been mulling over the idea of inaugurating an International match between England and Scotland and on the instruction of the Club Council Harold Janion, the Secretary, wrote a letter to the Editors of the principal newspapers on 7th January stating that they proposed to invite ten gentlemen from each country to represent their country in a thirty-six hole singles match at Royal Liverpool to be played on 26 April, this being immediately prior to the Amateur. Furthermore, they had asked the following gentlemen to select the teams. For Scotland:- B. Hall Blyth (Chairman of Rules of Golf committee), J.E. Laidlay (Amateur Champion 1889, 1891), J.L. Low (Captain of Oxford & Cambridge Golfing Society). For England:- H.H. Hilton (current Amateur Champion), H.G. Hutchinson (Amateur Champion 1886, 1887), Charles Hutchings (the Hoylake player). This surely was a clear mark of the respect in which Hutchings was held.

Although England lost the International match, Hutchings had taken 6 holes off Leslie Balfour Melville, and was probably feeling in good heart when the Amateur started on his own links. After disposing of J.M. Williamson from Royal Musselburgh by 6 and 5, he then had a good scalp beating Horace Hutchinson by

4 and 3 in the second round. In the fourth round Hutchings met J.A.T. Bramston of Oxford University — Bramston had played fifth for England in the preceding International match and was a powerful young man, fancied to do well and a rising star. Hutchings got through 4 and 2 and then beat V.A. Pollock from Felixstowe to reach the semi-final against James Robb of St. Andrews, a successful member of the Scottish team.

It was a close match with Hutchings having the better of the long game, and Robb the short game. The golf was scrappy for the first 9 holes, at which point Hutchings was one down. He was three down after 12 holes, but rallied so strongly that he took the next 5 holes to win by 2 and 1. In admiring his resolution in recovering so well, bear in mind also that this was his sixth match in quick succession, following also the 36 holes single in the International match. At 53 years old, the legs might reasonably have been complaining.

Hutchings' opponent in the Final, Sydney Fry, was comparatively new to the game. Writing about the finalist in the *Sporting Chronicle,* Horace Hutchinson said that Fry had only been playing for six or seven years. Furthermore, he was nearly 30 years old when he took up the game, had a handicap of 13 on joining Royal Mid Surrey, was down to 3 in 6 months and scratch before the year was out.

Hutchings was a skilful billiards player but remarkably Fry was an even better one and had won the Amateur Championship at billiards — he went on to win the Amateur Championship Cup presented by Messrs Orme outright when he won again in 1903. Another significant factor in this Amateur, and indeed the Open of the same year, was the coming of the Haskell ball at the expense of the gutta percha — the gutty. Horace Hutchinson writing in his book *50 Years of Golf* recalls that he first saw and played with the Haskell in 1891 when his brother-in-law brought some over from America and for a while he thought they were the only ones in the country. They then cost 2/6d as opposed to 1/- for the gutty, itself no mean price. The Haskell ball was much more volatile and could be driven further. However, it required a more sensitive touch around the greens. To quote Hutchinson again on the Amateur finalists "they were better able than most to adapt themselves to the new touch of the livelier balls for nearly all the competitors who used the Haskell were extremely good billiards players ... The sensitive fingers of these billiards players helped them to get the touch of these livelier balls which were so 'kittle' for the approach and putting."

The morning round was a triumph for Hutchings who went for all his shots. Overcoming a slight lapse on the first, which he lost, he played magnificent golf to be round in 75 and stand 8 up on Fry.

After six holes in the afternoon the margin remained at 8 up, though Hutchings' golf had not continued in the same rich vein as the morning. Fry then holed the Dowie, the Far and the Punch Bowl in 2, 4, 4 to win them all and turn five down. Next he won the Short Alps in 4 then the Rushes in 3 — two more back and only three behind with the Hoylake finish to come. After winning the Lake in 5, Fry was short in two at the Dun with Hutchings on for two and the match could have finished there, near the Clubhouse. However, Fry pitched up over the cross-bunker which guarded the green and holed for his 4 and Hutchings, after a lazy first putt, holed an awkward second to remain two ahead. Fry's good 4 won the Royal and so to the Stand where both were on for two. Fry made sure of his 4 and from some 8 yards Hutchings played a weak approach putt, no nearer than 3 yards, from where he holed out for victory to the acclamation of the large crowd containing his wife, three daughters and so many of his local friends.

Winning the Amateur was the pinnacle of his career and gave great satisfaction to the player, his family and friends at Hoylake.

He moved from Hoylake in 1906 to Arle, a village just outside Cheltenham, where he lived until his death in 1922. His grandson recalls visiting him there twice as a young boy but could not remember much of it except a huge orchard of Victoria plums and many roses, and I have read elsewhere that Hutchings was a keen rosarian even as a young man.

Hutchings lived the life of a well-to-do gentleman. From about the turn of the century he customarily wintered at Pau where he was an eminent member of Pau Golf Club and he led them to victory over their rivals, Biarritz, on six consecutive occasions. To celebrate this fact he was given a replica of the Pau–Biarritz Challenge Cup which is still in the possession of the family. Another delightful illustration of the age and circumstances in which he lived was that he was a particular friend of the Jameson family — the whiskey people in Ireland — and they sent him an annual present of 30 gallons of whiskey.

Charles Hutchings

It would be easy to think that Hutchings was overshadowed by the likes of Allan Macfie, Harold Hilton, John Ball Jnr., Horace Hutchinson and Jack Graham. Glancing through the records of the Royal Liverpool Medals during the two decades 1885–1905 would seem to add substance to this but I do not think it was really true. Hutchings' record on and off the links was most distinguished. Above all, to win the Amateur as a grandfather on his own links after participating in the event over a span of 18 years is a supreme achievement. He did not play in the Amateur again after winning — what a delightful way to finish — at the top!

The Grahams of Hoylake

Michael Marshall

As Bernard Darwin wrote "Golf seems to run in families at Hoylake"; in no family has it "run" so strongly as the Grahams.

Many articles have been written about individual members of the family but the purpose of this piece is to set down the story of the four Grahams who have been best known for their association with Hoylake and prowess at the game of golf.

John Graham Junior, as he is named in the list of Captains of the Club, came from Glasgow to Liverpool in 1873 — four years after the formation of the Club — when the family sugar-refining business moved to Liverpool. He was a strict Presbyterian teetotaller and according to his Captain's portrait in the club-room, a stern-looking bearded gentleman. He built The Croft in Stanley Road as the summer house for his family — the main dwelling was in Liverpool — and from there his three golfing children, Jack, Molly and Allan became familiar with the links upon which they were to become famous.

John Graham was a good and keen golfer, if not a great one. He took considerable interest in the affairs of the Club, was Captain in 1886/87 at the age of 42 and Council Minutes show him to be constructively contentious — not unlike his grandson John — and no doubt with the same twinkle in his eye. He it was who raised in Council the question whether, upon Queen Victoria's death in 1901 the Club was entitled to remain "Royal". The gratifying result of the subsequent enquiries was that King Edward VII "commanded that this be so".

Jack Graham, the elder son of John, was a very great player. Together with John Ball and Harold Hilton, he was the third member of the "Hoylake Triumvirate". Although overshadowed by Ball and Hilton and their performances in the Open and Amateur Championships, there is no doubt that his contemporaries thought he was capable of winning anything.

Jack

Bernard Darwin referred to him as "a player of unquestioned genius". At Hoylake, there is a match card of the first golf contest between America and Great Britain (subsequently the Walker Cup) setting out the names and order of play: on the opposite page under the date May 21st 1921 is inscribed "To Mr. John Graham, the father of the finest golfer there ever was" and signed by all the players. At that time, John Graham was seriously ill and indeed died a few days later on the eve of the final of the Amateur Championship in which his younger son Allan was beaten by W.I. Hunter.

Jack Graham, despite his obvious golfing

Molly

genius, never won the Amateur Championship. He was a better medal player than match player. His record testifies to that. He could win most of his International Matches, and always did well in the earlier rounds of the Championship. But the exhausting effort of the full week seemed too much for him. He just did not have the killer instinct, when it was needed, and under pressure his putting became suspect.

Nonetheless, his record is outstandingly impressive. Twenty-five gold and fourteen silver medals; a score of 66 in the year 1910 — an almost incredible figure for the conditions of the time; in the ten years he played for Scotland, he lost only two matches; five times he reached the semi-finals of the Amateur; he twice won the Gold Vase at St. Georges; in the Open he was leading amateur on five occasions.

He died at the age of 37 : killed at Hooge in 1915 leading his Company of the Liverpool Scottish. It is a singular recognition of his ability that all newspapers saw fit to print obituaries (at the time when obituaries were all too frequent) of considerable length. To quote yet again from Bernard Darwin: "He could not have left a more unforgettable or pleasanter memory."

Mary Allan Graham — Molly — was the younger sister of Jack. Born in 1880, she died in the 1950s. Apart from being an extraordinarily good golfer, she was a County tennis player, first-class rock-climber, badminton player and skater — a fistful of abilities!

At the age of 10 she won the Girls Competition at Hoylake, but when she grew up almost all her golf was played elsewhere — ladies had no place in golf at Hoylake until after the 1939/45 war. She was a member of Moreton Golf Club — in those days (pre 1914–18 war) a popular and thriving Club. Many of the Hoylake members were also members of Moreton since Moreton permitted Sunday play whilst Hoylake did not.

Molly won many Gold Medals at Moreton, several of which now make up a bracelet worn today by Avril Graham, the wife of her nephew John. She won both the British Ladies Championship and the Scottish Ladies Championship and was runner-up in the former once and the latter twice.

The British win took place at Aberdovey and earned the headline in *The Scotsman* of 28th May 1901: "An unfortunate incident at the Ladies Championship". In the semi-final round between Molly Graham and Mrs. Stanley Stubbs, the referee announced the 8th hole as halved in 7. Neither player protested and they played on. At the 10th, some of the spectators told the referee that the 8th had not been halved but Molly had won it with a 7. The referee said that since neither

Allan

player had questioned his decision at the time, the 8th hole remained a half. The match was won 1 up by Mrs. Stubbs. The Championship Committee then took evidence from the spectators and decided that Molly had won the eighth and ordered the players to play on. Molly Graham won and went on to win the Championship.

Molly did not play seriously after the 1914–18 war, but in 1939 she did manage to beat her nephew John (then plus 1) by 9 and 8. Not unreasonably he says "She was the best golfer of the lot."

Allan James Graham — Allan — was the younger brother of Jack and Molly. While at Trinity College, Oxford, he first played golf for the University in 1903 and afterwards Captained the University side. After coming down from Oxford he qualified as a solicitor and became a highly respected international and shipping lawyer. He worked and lived at West Hartlepool and in 1911 won the Durham Championship. On the outbreak of the 1914–18 war he was called up in the Liverpool Scottish, but was very shortly pulled out by the Government to go to Copenhagen, where he spent the war trying to prevent the Danes shipping strategic materials to Germany.

He was a very good golfer and reached the final of the Amateur Championship at Hoylake in 1921 (having beaten Bobby Jones by 6 and 5 on the way) but, as mentioned earlier, was beaten in the final, having had to go onto the first tee on that May morning knowing that his father had died the night before.

Allan played for Scotland against England in 1925, and won a number of gold medals at Hoylake and other prizes. He was one of the first persons to be invited to be a member of the Hittite Golfing Society.

He was Captain of the Club in 1924 at the age of 40 : the youngest Captain Hoylake has had. Sadly he died in 1941 at the early age of 58, and Bernard Darwin on his death wrote of "a kindly flavour of his own, gentle and yet very shrewd, and a particular twinkle".

John Allan Graham — John — the son of Allan, nephew of Jack and Molly, grandson of John Graham from Glasgow — against the background of his forbears was bound to be an exceedingly good golfer and he was — and is.

He started young and in 1931 won the Boys Medal (over 15 and under 18) with a record 77 and his father Allan, having won the same Medal in 1897, created a father and son record, equalled only by the Farrar family.

From the date of his full membership of the Club, his record is extraordinary. Between 1937 and 1961 (with no competitions for 1940-45 inclusive) he won 30

John

major Club competitions — and for good measure, three more in 1971 and 1973. He also won the Captain's Prize twice.

So far as golf outside Hoylake was concerned, he had a Walker Cup trial in 1938; won the Cheshire foursomes twice and was runner-up once; and made numerous appearances for Cheshire; played for a number of years for Marlborough in the Halford Hewitt, including a year in which they won; won at least once each of the major competitions of the Hittites. On becoming a senior in 1970 he played for the Seniors against the American and Canadian Seniors in Canada and again two years later at Royal Birkdale.

John was Captain of Hoylake in 1956 at the age of 41, thereby creating a remarkable record of three successive generations of direct descent being Captain. The oldest on election, was John's grandfather, aged 42.

He has a remarkably fluent and attractive swing, which age has not flawed. His one chink is the very short putt, but we all have our weak spot, although in such a good golfer it is difficult to believe it should be so.

The versatile sporting achievements of Molly Graham — not only golf but tennis, skating, etc., all have been mentioned, but little said of the versatility in sport of Jack, Allan and John. The reason is that they were all astonishingly similar, not only in sporting achievement but in looks and character. Each was a first-class ball player — outside golf, at tennis, racquets and any other game or sport requiring a quick eye and a sure touch; each was tall and lithe — not truly the ideal stature for a first class golfer, as we are given to understand in the year 1990, but nevertheless it seemed to serve its purpose.

Froes Ellison

John Rees Roberts

If we could turn the clock back to the year 1925 and walk over the links at Royal Liverpool, we might come across the tall and handsome T.F. Ellison. To everyone at Hoylake he was known as "Froes" and was as complete a golfer and athlete as could be found anywhere. In his history of Royal Liverpool, the late Guy Farrar described "Froes" as the best player that Hoylake had produced since the Great War.

Born in 1894 at West Kirby of wealthy parents, he was schooled at Sedbergh where success came at sport including a victory in the renowned Wilson run, a

Froes Ellison

10 mile race across the fells. During school holidays at Hoylake he spent many hours learning the game of golf, at which he was to excel.

He was of the generation which was drawn into the great conflict of World War I, and he served as an Infantry Officer with the Royal Northumberland Fusiliers — "The Fighting 5th" — happily returning unscathed. He then joined his father on the cotton market in Liverpool. His golfing achievements might have been even greater had the war not interrupted him at an age when he was already showing great promise.

Froes was a man of spare build, giving an impression that he was all wire and whipcord. His blue, deep set and penetrating eyes, made a formidable impact on any opponent at the first tee. Although the age of the plus-foured golfer was in vogue, he was rarely seen on the links in anything save slacks, with a well-cut tweed jacket of the sort Abe Mitchell always favoured. There were no such things in those days as waterproof over-clothes and when it rained Froes merely turned up his jacket collar, shrugged his shoulders and got on with his game, totally disregarding the drenching he was getting.

From Farrar, we have an accurate account of his golfing technique. His back swing was short and with a long follow through he hit the ball a powerful blow but without the "timing" essential for very long driving. When he did hit his drives well there was little chance for any opponent, but perhaps because of his uncertainty with the wooden clubs, particularly off the tee, success sometimes eluded him. The strength of his game lay in his iron play. His long irons were superb, and this in the days of the hickory shaft when the club could be turned fractionally by the turf to send the ball many degrees off the intended line.

Like John Ball, Froes was a bold putter, giving the hole a chance but unlike his more famous senior, he invariably holed "the back one". Farrar's final comment was a compliment of the highest quality when he stated that, from John Ball, Froes had inherited some of the "will to win" and shared with him the ability to extricate himself from awkward situations by some master stroke produced at the critical moment in the match. "Ellison is always most dangerous when he is tucked up in a bunker, with his opponent on the green. Out comes the ball, down goes the putt, and his adversary, if he has neglected the simple precaution of laying his approach putt dead, is left with a nasty one for the half. I have seen him 'break up' the opposition, time after time in this way."

Before we recount the details of his golfing achievements, let us digress from golf briefly to remind ourselves of his superb athleticism in other fields of sport. His friend, Wrayford Willmer a Member of this Club until his death quite recently, told a story of a famous wager Ellison made. This unusual exploit took place in March 1926.

I shall let Wrayford Willmer tell the story:

> It began in the compartment of a railway carriage on an evening train from Birkenhead Woodside to Chester in February 1926. Six young business men were on their way home to Chester from their jobs in various Liverpool offices, when one of their number told his fellow travellers that he knew the two men from the Cotton Market who had recently walked from Liverpool to Chester. From the other corner the view was expressed that that was not a very spectacular feat and that it would have been something to boast about if they had run the 20 miles. Another man supported this view and discussion ensued which culminated in a challenge being thrown down to the two who had spoken.
>
> This was how it happened that T.F. Ellison, with his friend W.F. Beavan, well known in the Property market, ran the 20 miles from Hoylake to Chester on 28th March 1926. They had both seen considerable service as Infantry Officers in the First War, when physical fitness was essential to survive, and they had both been at Sedbergh, renowned for the Wilson Run — in which they had both competed and was in fact won one year by Ellison. When the bets were made they were given about a month to train for the event. The time fixed for the run was 2 hours 45 minutes, but there were a variety of other bets including one which involved Froes Ellison only — that after the run, but on the same day, he would play a round over the Old Chester Golf Club's course

at Sealand in 75 strokes or less.

28th March was a Sunday, and the run was timed to start at 6.00 am. Traffic in those days was very light and early on a Sunday morning almost non-existent. For some obscure reason I was roped in as timekeeper, my only hardship being that I had to drive over from Chester to Hoylake at that unseemly hour in my snub-nosed Morris Cowley. I followed the runners all the way back to Chester and certified the time taken as 2 hours 31 minutes. The run itself was uneventful so far as I remember, but I am sure that there must have been moments when one or both of the runners wished that they had not started this trial of strength and fitness. They finished the run on the steps of the Grosvenor Hotel, winning what was then quite a lot of money. We all breakfasted in the Grosvenor and then Ellison went on to Sealand where he proceeded to play his usual immaculate golf and win his side-bet with something to spare. It had to be Sealand, by the way, because in those days it was the only Club in the district to permit play on Sundays.

Back to his golfing achievements. The facts that he played for England against Scotland in 1922 and again between 1925 and 1927, and that he won 15 Gold and 3 Silver medals at Hoylake are scarcely important; nor that he had only moderate success in the British Amateur Championship — his best performance in the five times that he competed was his first, at Muirfield in 1920, where he reached the last 16.

Pride of place in the story of Froes Ellison must go to the accounts of his greatest golfing triumphs. In 1925 the English Golf Union inaugurated the English native (or close) Championship on the links of Royal Liverpool, with the Club donating the handsome trophy for the event. It was natural that there was a strong entry, which included three past Amateur Champions — John Ball, by that time 63 years old — E.A. Lassen of Bradford, playing almost unnoticed — and the majestic Cyril Tolley, who drew the largest gallery. Only Holderness and Wethered, both winners of the Amateur Championships were missing from the draw sheet.

The meeting began on 22nd April, with Tolley the firm favourite and much of what the golfing correspondent of *The Liverpool Daily Post* wrote on that day and on the two that followed was a full description of his exploits. It came as a surprise to him and to everyone, that he was beaten by 2 holes by Sam Robinson of Southport and Ainsdale in the quarter-final. Robinson was a good golfer, the Lancashire Champion in 1914, and as we shall see, was to contest the final of this first English Championship with courage, fine play and great sportsmanship.

Significantly the first mention of Froes Ellison by *The Liverpool Post*'s golfing scribe did not appear until the second day of the tournament when Froes beat successively two Internationals — Carl Bretherton and R.A. Montmorency. It was clear that the morning encounter was the more keenly contested, Froes having to hole his fourth shot at the 9th — with a mashie — for a half while Bretherton was already on the green in 2! Froes played tighter golf on the homeward half, and with 4s at the 14th and 16th holes won by 2 and 1.

Next day Ellison defeated Squadron-Leader Hayward in the morning round. He averaged level 4s for 13 holes but then fell away to win eventually by only one hole. His semi-final match against H.L. Holden was something of an anticlimax, and he won easily.

The other semi-final was also rather a tame affair with Sam Robinson defeating Israel Sidebottom, the prince of "wagglers" by 5 and 4. The latter's swing began with a sedate and slow pendulum movement, which worked up to a crescendo of waggles, before the ball was finally struck.

Those of us privileged to play our golf at Hoylake will have no difficulty in picturing the morning of the final day, Friday 24 April; as ever, a west wind was blowing, a great advantage, so it would seem, to a player with Froes Ellison's local knowledge. It was not to be so — Sam Robinson saw to that.

The Liverpool Post's headlines on the following day read "New Champion's grim final at Hoylake". At no stage in the 36 hole match were the finalists separated by more than two holes and for long periods they were all square.

Losing the first two holes, level after five, Froes was never down again until the 28th. There with three-quarters of the match gone, at the Dee, Ellison lost a hole he should have won. The next five holes were halved but at the Dun (16th), measuring 525 yards, he got a great 4 by holing from 8 feet to square the match. At the Royal, Robinson's putt for a 4 stayed out, Ellison having already settled for a 5 — the strain was beginning to tell, and so to the home hole with the match level.

Ellison drove down the middle, and Robinson into heavy rough on the right of the fairway, from where he struck a spoon which hit the green only to shoot across to the rough beyond. Ellison with a cleek, found the green, but was 20 yards short of the pin, so he was the first to play, and his well-judged putt finished a yard from the hole. Robinson's little chip was 8 feet short; now everything depended on his putt which peeped into the hole but eventually decided to stay out. Froes Ellison made no mistake with his yarder and "amid great enthusiasm" became the first native English Champion.

No one will dispute that this first victory in the English Championship was the greatest achievement in Froes Ellison's golfing life. He was to find the going easier in the September of the following year, when he successfully defended his title at Walton Heath. His victories in the earlier rounds of this second English Championship were by narrow margins and in the 5th round against H.V. Mathews of Worthing, he found that his erratic tee shots left him in the heather and he only scraped home on the 17th hole by holing a putt of 20 yards to win. Unlike the "dog fight" of 1925, this second final, against Squadron Leader C.H. Hayward, Champion of the Royal Air Force successively from 1921 to 1924, proved to be a one way affair. Ellison began strongly, 3 up after six holes, and gathered strength being 8 up by the 15th with a score of level 4s. He lunched 7 up.

In the afternoon the R.A.F. man made a spirited fight and although holes continued to be "traded" Ellison's long lead proved too much and eventually he won by 6 and 4. The sceptics who thought that he had been a fortunate winner of the first English Championship the year before had received a most fitting rebuttal.

No one will dispute that the name of Froes Ellison can be added to those of the great Triumvirate of Royal Liverpool — Ball, Hilton and Graham — as one more of the great sons of Hoylake.

Gladys Ravenscroft

Betty Lloyd

Born in 1888, Gladys began playing golf on holiday at Rhosneigr with her father, and later joined Formby Ladies Golf Club where her name is on the boards. Her father was first and foremost a cricketer but later took up golf and became Captain of Formby during the 1920s.

Gladys had played hockey at school, and achieved a place in the Cheshire side, before turning to the Royal and Ancient game. She then became a member of Bromborough Golf Club and was coached by the professional, Fred Robson. He soon told her that she could not hope to improve her golf until she gave up hockey. This she did and by 1909 was the second reserve for England, when the matches were played at Birkdale. This was immediately prior to the British Ladies Championship, in which she reached the fifth round. She was beaten by a former bronze medallist.

The Tatler of June 30th 1909 reports as follows:

> Miss Ravenscroft, from the Bromborough Golf Club, whence comes that splendid professional Ginger Robson, was undoubtedly the "flapper" of the 1909 Championship. She started in the first round by taking Miss F. Walker-Leigh, one of the soundest of Irish players, to the 19th green and winning there. Next, she astonished everyone by beating Miss L. Moore of whose play great things are said, and who was expected to go a long way through the tournament. Then, Mrs. Whitehead was a victim and after adding Miss D. Tucker, a well-known Surrey County player to her scalps, she was beaten by Mrs. Sumpter only on the seventeenth green. Surely a splendid record in a first championship.

Gladys became an International in 1911 and the following year became established on the International scene. She won the British Ladies Championship at Turnberry, was a finalist in the French Championship, and won the Cheshire Ladies Championship for the first of seven occasions.

After becoming British Ladies Champion, Gladys received many telegrams of congratulation notable among which was one from her father. It read, "Good old Gladys, delighted, David is dining with me to celebrate. Hope you will feel fit after the exertion, and mother no worse for excitement. Proud Father."

Gladys in 1913—American Champion

Sir William Lever, later to become Lord Leverhulme, gave a dinner party in her honour at Thornton Manor.

In 1913 Gladys was to reach the peak of her golf career. Along with other British golfers she crossed the Atlantic, and played in Ottawa and Montreal, before travelling to Wilmington Country Club for the United States Women's National Championship. She became the first English player to win this coveted title. Fellow Cheshire player Muriel Dodd won the Canadian title, and so the two Cheshire girls were feted as they toured the U.S.A., then feted again on their return to England and Bromborough Golf Club.

Gladys continued her international golf until 1914, and again after the Great War, in 1920 and 1921, 1925 and finally in 1930.

Her seventh and last Cheshire Championship came in 1928. Amazingly, she reached the final in 1948 and 1949 at the age of 60.

Gladys played all her international golf as a member of Bromborough Golf Club, and today her portrait hangs in the club house to mark her international fame, and election as the first honorary life member of the Club in 1912. Sir William Lever commissioned the portrait in oils by Frank Copnall.

In 1915 Gladys married Lieutenant Temple Dobell, after a lightning engagement of little more than three weeks. The wedding took place at St. Martin's-in-the-Fields, London. In the following nine years, Temple and Gladys had four children. The eldest, Barbara, later to become Bah Nottingham, played a full part in the "County" and Veterans society, and also as a life-long member of Bromborough Golf Club. She, too, has been elected an honorary life member of Bromborough Golf Club. This was in 1987, 75 years after her mother.

From an early age Gladys had been a permit-holder of the Royal Liverpool a title then given to the female relatives of members. This allowed them the facility to play golf, but little more. Gladys would be taken to the Club by her father, she would change her shoes in the car, and proceed to the 1st tee via the caddies' entrance. On quiet days, the Secretary would invite Mr. Ravenscroft to bring his daughter into his office for a cup of tea. She would then leave the building — via the caddies' entrance. When Gladys told me this story in the early 1950s, she capped it by saying that she thought she would live to see the day when Royal Liverpool had L.G.U. tees. Time proved her to be right. In 1958 they formed a ladies club, to be known as Hilbre Ladies Golf Club. The "permit holders" then met to choose their first Captain. Gladys Dobell was invited, and accepted what was to become one of the final crowns in her distinguished career.

In the last ten years or so of her life, Gladys was an enthusiastic club golfer. During this time I frequently met her playing inter-club matches. She presented an imposing sight standing on the tee and made a daunting opponent. When it was her turn to drive, she would stand on the tee and give the ground a firm blow with the sole of her driver. This was an indication to her caddie as to where she would like him to tee up the ball. She still struck the ball with enormous authority, with her two-handed grip and the right hand curiously underneath the shaft of the club. Her putting too, was unusual. With her "old friend" of a steel-bladed,

1958 Cheshire Ladies Championship—Mrs Temple Dobell (Hilbre Ladies Captain) standing second right

hickory-shafted putter, she attacked the hole in a way rarely seen: the ball would hit the back of the hole, jump in the air and finally drop in. There was no floating the ball into the hole for Gladys. During these years she became a great source of advice and help for the young golfer, and I count myself lucky to have benefited from her wisdom.

She regarded her golf as total fun, and a great adventure, but was at the same time a great competitor. Wherever she was, there would be laughter in abundance, and her favourite motto was: "It counts not how you win or lose but how you play the game."

Charles Timmis

Leslie Edwards

Froes Ellison, it has been suggested, was Hoylake's finest golfer in the 1920s. Charlie Timmis can lay claim to that distinction in the 1930s.

It was in 1926, as a junior member of Leasowe, that he first came to prominence, reaching the final of the Boys Championship at Coombe Hill, but losing narrowly to E.A. McRuvie. He was soon making his name at senior level, winning competitions at Leasowe and then Royal Liverpool, where he became a member in 1930. As a teenager in 1928 he had tied for the Liverpool Golf Championship, then an important event in which most of the leading local professionals participated. He won the County Championship for the first time in 1934, and was to win it twice more after the war.

Working in the family provision trade business in Birkenhead meant that he had the time to play in the Amateur Championships. This was for him the highlight of the golfing calendar and he always prepared thoroughly for it, with plenty of practice, even reducing his tobacco and alcoholic intake for a few weeks before it. He reached the fifth round on two occasions and the sixth round once (at Hoylake in 1939). After the Championship each year he would turn his attention to cricket, his other great sporting love.

In 1936 and 1937 he represented England in the Home Internationals. He had played one match in 1930. In those two years he did not lose a single; one was halved and all the others won. Despite this record he was thought to be a better stroke player than match player, as the records of Medal winners at Hoylake bear testimony. His name appears 29 times in all, and how many more times that might have been but for the lost years of the war. He also won the John Ball Putter (the Hittite Golfing Society Championship) on four occasions.

Whilst his style of play is best remembered for the habit of shifting his weight from left foot to right and back again just before the start of his back swing, he had an elegant swing, full and with a wide arc. The best part of his game was his wooden-club play. He drove far and straight. Following the Cheshire Championship on one occasion, he chided his friend Bruce Thompson about his driving — "You know Bruce, you need to drive straight. I only missed one fairway

Charles Timmis

through the Championship" — and that was two qualifying rounds and four of match play. His fairway woods, flighted high, were equally good and this gave him many opportunities of saving shots at the long holes. As for his putting, despite a tendency to move on them, he holed more than his share. Hours of competitive putting in front of the Clubhouse, often "accumulators" with Norman Fogg and Bruce Thompson, taught him the hard way.

Those who knew him however remembered him not so much for his golfing achievements, as for his character. When, as Captain-elect of Royal Liverpool, having just completed a year as President of the Cheshire Union of Golf Clubs he died at the age of 43, I wrote this tribute to him for the *Liverpool Echo,* under the heading "Noble in Play: Nobler in Character".

> Words cannot measure this loss, nor can they measure the affection in which the man was held, not only at Hoylake but everywhere his noble character and sportsmanship shone from the sunny, gentle disposition. He was loved, not because he played cricket, golf, and rugby football, so well and so easily, but because he always lost as gracefully as he won and because the game, and the fun he took from it, was the thing he counted above all. Everyone liked him. The enormity of his death so young will be felt no less keenly by the caddies, with their unerring valuation of people, than by members of his club and golfers everywhere in the North.
>
> I count it a privilege to have known him since his schoolboy days. In thirty years of watching and writing sport I know of no one who so captivated friend, foe and spectator by his fairness, his perfect deportment and his ability as a player.
>
> Yet through the pattern of his life ran a recurring thread of misfortune, culminating in the greatest tragedy of all. As a boy he was so badly concussed it was thought his Rugby career was ended. Later, he played for Birkenhead Park, but he had to forsake the game as a result of his earlier injury.
>
> Then there was the double tragedy of the war years. When his cricket and golf should have been giving him years of pleasure, he was serving with the Royal Horse Artillery in North Africa. He endured the siege of Tobruk, but the germ of an obscure disease, Addison's, was to prove the more fatal enemy.
>
> Years after the war, when he was winning the last of his three Cheshire

championships, a doctor friend discerned the illness which ended his hopes of further competitive golf, and of playing again for England.

Charles Timmis bore this life sentence with the stoicism and philosophy one expected from him. Injections enabled him to play an occasional round of golf, and lack of practice did not prevent him from continuing to be an opponent to be feared. His friends delighted as he did, in this ability to snatch a game or two, and, this being Amateur Championship year at Hoylake, who better to grace the Captain's chair? He was to have been installed a week next Saturday. One thing ever prevented Charles Timmis from winning a national title — the lack of what is known as the "killer" instinct. In medal play he was superb. In hand-to-hand combat it seemed that holing a long putt (and he holed many) hurt him more than it did his opponent.

No one could imagine Charles Timmis winning by 6 and 4 if it were possible for him to win, instead by 3 and 2. His kindly nature came out in this and other ways, and we shall never cease to be grateful to him for trying to show, in this material age, that winning matches and championships should be subservient to good sportsmanship and companionship. Cheshire champion, runner-up in a boys' championship, co-first in the Liverpool championship with the late Ronald Vickers ... cricketer with Birkenhead Park and Neston ... Rugby player with Birkenhead Park, Charles Timmis and his wonderful qualities can never slip from the memory of his countless friends.

He rates with Hoylake immortals, John Ball, Harold Hilton, Jack Morris and Jack Graham, not because his golf was outstanding but because his supremely unselfish, quiet nature made him everyone's friend.

His epitaph, for me, must always be: Noble in Play — Nobler in Character.

The Doctor

Leslie Edwards

There was nothing about his physique to suggest that Dr John Lawrie was a good golfer. He was heavily built, burly — incapable, it seemed, of athletic movement. He had a leonine head set deep into his shoulders. He had style, and it showed. It was almost unthinkable that he should go out without a caddy. The ball teed, he surveyed the shot from a few yards behind it and strode to his stance so imperiously and with such panache one felt he was going to hit it at least 500 yards. He did hit the ball a long way and held one year the leading gold medal at St Andrews to prove it, but his *forte* was fairway woods. No professional could have hit them more impressively.

To everyone in golf here and in the United States he was known effectively as The Doctor. He'd served on the R and A Championship Committee: had been captain at Hoylake and had several times attended the Masters tournament in Augusta, promoted by his boyhood hero Bobby Jones. He considered Jones the finest golfer in the history of the game and the man every young golfer should try to emulate.

That he was condemned all his life to endure a stammer marked enough to daunt the bravest did not register with the Doctor. Indeed, in his worst moments of stress when he spoke publicly, it was the audience who suffered agonies of suspense while he wrestled silently (or as near silently as he could) to start a sentence. His indifference to this handicap was providential. If anything the stammer added point to what he said in that he was blessed with a lovely sense of humour.

When he came in from a match against the Oxford and Cambridge Society at Hoylake (and most of the club team that day had lost) John Graham asked him, "Did you win?" The Doctor said he had. "By how many?" enquired Graham. The answer after the inevitable jumble of incoherent sounds and head and stomach tilting was: "MMM — um — er — ummm-millions."

Yet he lacked nothing in shrewdness. Before the last round of the Open Championship at Troon in 1962 someone bet the Doctor five pounds that Palmer would not break 70. My abiding recollection of that day of melting heat is of John Lawrie marching at the head of Arnie's army of thousands of excited fans down the long sixth hole which few players were reaching with two woods, but which Palmer seemed to find the most commonplace of par fours.

When Palmer and his partner, Kel Nagle, played their second shots to the eighteenth green and Palmer was seen to be sailing serenely to an Open Championship triumph, the crowd broke ranks and stampeded on to the fairway to form a hollow square and get a closer look at the final putts. There was delay while the players and stewards struggled through massed spectators to reach the green. When order was restored Palmer, who faced a putt of several yards, sidled over to the Doctor and whispered, "What have I got to win, Doc?" The answer, because Palmer had been told of the five-pound bet, can hardly have surprised him: "Nnnn-um — um nnnever mmmm-ind about www-hat you've got to ww-in. Th-th-th-um-think of mmm-e and the www-ife and kids," said Lawrie. "Pppp-utt it in!"

And Palmer did.

The Doctor and Henry Longhurst in their playing days took advantage at St Andrews during an Amateur Championship of the splendid full-length driving range, now sadly part of the University precinct, which used to be run by the professional, MacAndrew. Each took two buckets of balls; each was intent on improving his driving; each bucket contained about fifty golf balls. Far from improving their driving got worse and worse. Shots flew off to all points on the horizon. It was hot work. Ultimately Longhurst completed his second bucket and rested, perspiring from his labour, while Lawrie flailed away on the adjoining tee. "How many have you got left?" Longhurst demanded. The Doctor, red-faced, exhausted, frustrated almost beyond words answered ruefully: "Only ttt-en — um — more ... Th-ank God!"

There was another famous moment at Formby when the Doctor, refereeing a match between Michael Bonallack and the American Downing Gray in the Amateur Championship, was asked at the Punchbowl green of the thirteenth: "Whose play?" Bonallack's ball was barely on the front edge of the green; Gray's lay high on the bank on the left. The Doctor walked to the flag and there made his decision. Gray was not happy about it and asked for a measurement. This involved the Doctor in paced journeys to and from both balls and took a considerable time.

As he walked the final few yards uphill to Gray's ball his three-foot stride suddenly began to contract to something nearer two feet nine inches. All this time some 200 spectators were standing in respectful silence. There was then a moment of hiatus. The Doctor's decision refused to come. Finally it arrived in a burst: "Ah-um-ahb-er-solutely eee-qual!" They spun for it and Bonallack, if my memory is correct, eventually won a fine match at the twentieth. The gallery was still chuckling five minutes after the Doctor's decision, but it did not bother him a bit. He'd done his job. If there was any fun to be had from anything he had said or done, all the better.

I am sure the Doctor would happily have used, for his own purposes, the crack which none of us made during his lifetime and which I make now only in the sure knowledge that he will greet it, in the Elysian fields, with a chuckle: "Me? I'm the original inarticulated Lawrie!"

(from *The Golfers* edited by P. Dobereiner, published by Collins 1982)

Jos

John Graham

Not very long ago a man came up to Jos and said "Good God! Are you really Ionicus? I thought you had gone years ago." Let me assure that person that Joshua Charles Armitage, alias Ionicus, is not only alive but is carrying on his art in the same way that he has done for nearly forty years, and, as far as I can see, he will continue to do so for many years to come. But, before we discuss his successes, let us consider some basic facts. Jos was born, almost blind in the left eye, on 26th September 1913 at Hoylake where he has lived ever since. He went to school at the Hoylake Parade Central Higher Elementary School, progressing to the Liverpool School of Art after which he became a teacher of art in Liverpool. He married Catherine Buckle in May 1939 and has two daughters. Sadly his wife died in 1985.

During the war he volunteered for the Navy. At his medical he was asked to read the letters on a chart with his hand over his left eye. That was easy. He was then asked to cover his right eye. He left a slight gap between the two middle fingers enabling him to read the letters, and he was in the Royal Navy as a signaller! The trouble was that a year or two later he applied for a Commission. This time, at his medical, the doctor placed a card over each eye in turn and, of course, that was that. He was given a job as an instructor on aircraft recognition. During this period he sent ten drawings to *Punch.* They retained one and he has been doing work for them ever since.

His early work in 1944 included some Ionic columns in the background and, because he was interested in architectural drawing, he thought that Ionicus would be a suitable pseudonym. He decided to become a self-employed artist in 1950. He describes his art as humorous water-colour drawings and strenuously denies that he is a cartoonist. "After all", he once told me, "I do not make people's noses three inches longer than they should be." During the last forty years or so he has had some wonderful successes. He has illustrated 57 of P.G. Wodehouse paperbacks. Two of these, *Heart of a Goof* and *Uneasy Money,* were golfing illustrations. He has also illustrated a host of books by E.F. Benson (author of the Mapp and Lucia series on TV), Elizabeth Goudge, Aldous Huxley, Ogden Nash (the American poet), *The Adventures of Pinnochio* by Carlo Colledi and many others. He is a perfectionist and spends much time in "getting it exactly right". In his opinion the best work he has ever done was when the United Oxford and Cambridge University Club in Pall Mall, London, commissioned twelve water-colour drawings of the exterior and interior of the Club. He has also contributed to the *Daily Mirror, The London Evening Standard* and the Yorkshire magazine, *The Dalesman.* His association with *Punch* brought him into contact with various notables. One of these was Malcolm Muggeridge, who, for a period, was editor. Jos regarded him as a bit pontifical. He very much admired another editor, Kenneth Bird ("Fougasse", the celebrated cartoonist), who created the wartime "Careless Talk Costs Lives" posters.

Jos is not, as some members of Hoylake may think, just an artist who paints humorous golfing scenes. He does that and does it exceedingly well. Many members have the good fortune to have one of these scenes hanging at home. For a number of years the first prize to the winners of the Hoylake Open Scratch Mixed Foursomes has been a pair of distinctive paintings, and they have proved highly acceptable. He was commissioned by Robert Halsall, the well-known Royal Birkdale professional, to produce six prints for a brochure celebrating the 100th Open Championship there in 1971. In this brochure Henry Longhurst wrote:

> What a happy thought to celebrate the 100th Open Championship with a set of prints calculated to adorn the walls both of Golf Clubs and the homes of dedicated golfers! The present set by Ionicus is a worthy successor to others of the past, which I myself have seen in Clubs not only at home but as far afield as Australia, South Africa and many parts of the United States, the sight of which not only makes the roving player feel at home but at the same time reminds him of the universal cameraderie of golf.

What a lovely tribute to a fine artist by a fine writer.

Jos has an impish sense of fun. It tickles him to think that he is probably the oldest full-time working member in the Club. His hobbies are gardening, golf and piano playing. He tends his small garden with great care. Although he has less than ten square metres of lawn, he regularly consults the Hoylake greenkeeper, Mr Green, about it.

He learnt his golf before the war on the Hoylake Municipal Golf Course and had always wanted to belong to the Royal Liverpool. It was a proud moment, he told me, when he was elected a member in 1962. Being a traditionalist, he feels that the Club may now be in danger of losing its aura. His lowest handicap was 12, against 22 today. During his membership he has won the Captain's Prize (red course) in 1965. He has won the aggregate prize for the Autumn Meeting (green course) and also the Orme Cup. He prefers "foursomes" and does not particularly like "fourballs" and it is his great disappointment that he has never won a "foursome" competition.

He plays the piano well and when he is playing some of those wonderful "oldies" he has a style reminiscent of Charlie Kunz. Although he can read music a little, he plays mainly by ear. His handwriting is just about the best that I have seen these days. One can immediately understand why he is such a meticulous artist.

To sum up, I commend the judgement of an ex-Captain who vetted Jos on his application to join Royal Liverpool. He reported to Council "I cannot think of a better person to be a member of the Club than the candidate."

Michael Pearson

Leslie Edwards

Of all the notable golfers who have been members of the Royal Liverpool club over the past 35 years — among them Ronnie White, Brian Chapman, Robin Biggs, Graham Brown and Dr. Blyth Bell — none has earned such affection from fellow-members as Michael Pearson. Most of them know him merely as one who is seen at the club on Sunday mornings. They may well appreciate that he has been a first-class player and indeed that he is still a fine golfer, but they have little knowledge of his record or of what has made him one of the nicest, most modest, characters we possess. I must add that no matter where one goes among golfers in the North-West, or even nationally, that opinion holds good. He is one of those rarities, a man with no enemies and many admirers.

Michael learned his golf as boy at Prenton where one of the Jarman brothers, Bob, set his swing permanently in the right groove. His first effort in the British Boys' Championship must have delighted Jarman as he reached the fifth round at Bruntsfield in 1946, after beating Guy Wolstenholme, later an English Champion, by one hole. Peter Alliss, like Michael was one of the last eight and both had played for England in the Boys' internationals.

In pre-War days Michael's first love was gymnastics. His coach in Birkenhead was the legendary Charlie Lord, a former member of the British Olympic team.

It was after he had done his National Service in the R.A.F. that Michael became, in 1949, a member of the Royal Liverpool club. His greatest fan and follower from the moment he gave notice that he had great golf potential was the then Secretary, Guy Farrar. He knew everything about greenkeeping, about photography and about Royal Liverpool traditions and customs and Pearson could not have had better advice as to how the game should be played and how the player, whatever his talent, should behave. Farrar's reading of Pearson's potential was rewarded in every respect in Guy's lifetime.

The disadvantages Michael Pearson suffered when his game was at its peak were self-inflicted. He worked in the family business and when his father died it was left to him to carry on single-handed. Thus, time and again, he was not able to spare time to play in the Amateur Championship or the native championship or in such events as the Brabazon or even some of the Cheshire county championships.

On two rare occasions when he was able to play in the Brabazon he finished joint second, in 1954 and again the following year, the winner on each occasion being Philip Scrutton. He played twelve times for England in the Home Internationals. In addition to his three victories in the Cheshire championship, Michael was twice runner-up. In 1952 David Shone beat him in the final and in 1969 he lost, in a play-off, at Hoylake against D.P. Jones of Bromborough. In one of the earlier rounds on this occasion he holed the Orchard hole in two shots, much to the delight of the Club's Centenary year Captain, Mr Selwyn Lloyd. The play-off against Jones had its moment of dire tragedy. At the Dowie short hole Pearson

Cheshire Championship final 1952—Michael with Guy Farrar and David Shone (winner)

struck four shots out of bounds and played nine from the tee! He fought back so magnificently that he was in contention again by the time they reached the fifteenth.

In more than one Amateur championship at Hoylake he has seemed set to reach the last four, or better, but a second shot out of bounds at the sixteenth virtually cost him the match against Rodney Foster in the fourth round in 1962 and a Scot, W.C. Davidson, beat him in the sixth round in 1969 largely as the result of a holed chip from "nowhere" for a two at the fourth where Pearson lay safe, as he thought, for a certain two.

At Ganton in a later Amateur Championship Michael lost to a strong American player named Thornton. Thornton's wife was in the gallery and when I explained to her that Pearson's Club was at Hoylake she said: "Gee, and to think that I've got a picture of your famous Alps hole at home on my mannel-shelf"! The following day when I met her and asked how her husband was faring she said, pointing some distance away at clumps of whins, "I don't know how he stands, but there he is with his bottom full of 'stickers'."

Michael Pearson is the quiet man of golf. He likes to hurry slowly. On the day of a competition he rises, shaves and breakfasts in leisurely style, and he tries to maintain that steady pace from the first tee to the last. No one displays a more equable temperament on the course, but it disguises a steely will which emerges when the occasion demands. Ask him to hole a putt which he considers is eminently holeable and, with tightened lips, he will answer you with a run of 3, 3, 4, 2, 3 or similar figures. His regret, like mine, is that golf is not what it was. The winners of Scratch medals, and he has won more that his share at Hoylake, Prenton and elsewhere, do not get the credit they deserve, so he maintains. The social side of golf and pro-ams seem almost to have become predominant.

His perfect balance and rhythm on the course, learnt perhaps from his early gymnastics, and carried through to his other great love — skiing — is equalled only by these same qualities when the game is over.

Down to the wire—Michael Pearson in 1969 Amateur

Campbell

Leslie Edwards

When writing of Michael Pearson, one can never dissociate him from his caddie and counsellor of 25 years and more — an exiled Scot, Alexander Campbell, who is now treading the Elysian fields and almost certainly seeking lost golf balls and anything else in the way of shining trivia which might attract his attention. Campbell, slightly stooped, swarthy, grizzled and nearly always perspiring — he wore a heavy coat, winter and summer — had started his caddying career in the 1920s when he carried mostly at Leasowe. It is a fact that when the Leasowe club professional, Billy Bee, played in the Open of 1923, at Troon, which Arthur Havers won, Campbell was at his master's hand to guide him to scores of 82, 81, 76, 83. But those scores did not represent the skill of the caddie. Moreover, in order to reach Troon, Campbell went by push bike, out and home.

Campbell's forehead, only rarely glimpsed because he always wore a dirty old cap, was as white as the rest of his face was grimy and weather-beaten and his black gypsy-type curls seemed always to be plastered down by sweat. At Christmas his invariable greeting to members of the club, many of whom provided him with his golfing wardrobe, was: "Arl the best, Mr. So-and-so, arl the best!" This seldom failed to produce the cost of a pint. On one occasion when there had been extensive structural alterations to the clubhouse the revered and fondly remembered "Nobby" Roberts said "I've just seen Campbell in Meols Drive en route to the station and, believe it or not, he's carrying one of the clubhouse doors on his back!"

At the time of the epidemic of thieving crows — they stole 23 balls on the morning of one competition — the club caused to be constructed a huge wire cage, like a large chicken coop, with a narrow entrance to tempt the crows to steal an assortment of old golf balls and small pieces of meat, and then find themselves trapped. Not a crow entered the portals, but Campbell was seen wandering round the cage looking longingly at the golf balls which he so devoutly wished were not out of bounds.

There was a time when Campbell was appointed, for a short period, caddie master, following the retirement of Steve Beck. Some American visitors who went to him to buy a few new balls — the pro's shop was closed for lunch — were turned away with a curt "Got no Dunlops: only 'effin Goblins!"

But he was expert at club selection; indeed he caddied for Allan Graham when that member of the great Hoylake family of golfers beat Bobby Jones by 6 and 5 in the Amateur. Campbell's sense of timing was never the equal of Michael Pearson's. There would be long putts which appeared to be destined for "half way" and Campbell would mutter angrily: " 'it it! 'it it!" as the ball rolled on relentlessly before it dropped gently into the hole. Then all was silence!

Michael thought he had done well to get rid of a difficult opponent in a tough championship match at Hoylake and when he finally nailed his man he said to Campbell "Well, what about that, Campbell?" "Aye," replied Campbell "but you shudder had the bracelets on 'im hours ago!" When he caddied for one of the leading players in a Brabazon at Hoylake I asked Campbell what kind of player he was. One gathered the man had putted somewhat indifferently. " 'im", said Campbell, "He couldn't putt butter on bread." Once in doubt as to whether he could find the last green with his second shot Pearson, after much cogitation, asked Campbell what he thought. The reply was as accurate as it was succinct "Give it timber, Mr. Pearson, give it timber..."

Campbell's propensity for picking up unconsidered trifles — silver paper, cartons, string, indeed anything which took his fancy (and that included many of the tees of people playing in fourball matches) — meant that his capacious overcoat pockets were always bulging with things he'd accumulated, not forgetting the odd kipper which he was taking home for tea or the £5 in silver which someone in the pro's shop had asked him to bring back from the bank in exchange for a white "fiver".

A great character and fondly remembered at Hoylake and Leasowe where towards the end of an interminable summer round ending at dusk Campbell was once heard to observe: "Been a bit slow, sir? Been a bit slow? Why, even the b— worms wuz overtaking us down the seventeenth!"

Pot Pourri

The Hoylake Medals

Guy Farrar

Writing about these medals is rather like taking a page out of golfing history, because during the first period of the Club's existence nearly every famous golfer in England, and a good many in Scotland, were at one time or another, members of the Royal Liverpool Golf Club. Long ago, each spring, a party of celebrated golfers used to begin at Westward Ho, come to Hoylake, and finish at St. Andrews, playing in each spring meeting in turn. In the autumn the order was reversed; the tour began at St. Andrews, and finished at Westward Ho. In those days subscriptions were nominal, and players joined a club in order to play for some particular prize. "The old order changeth," but two quaint customs remain to remind us of days long gone; the Hoylake meetings are always fixed to take place between the Westward Ho and the St. Andrews meetings, and the place of residence is always given after the names of the winners of these medals. No doubt with so many non-resident members playing, their place of residence helped the general public to identify them. The spring and autumn meetings were great gatherings in those days, with the southern golfers from Westward Ho and Blackheath, and the Scottish players from St. Andrews and Edinburgh.

These scratch prizes carry with them a gold or silver medallion, about the size of a shilling, as a memento, except the chief prize, the Club Gold Medal, which carries with it a large gold medallion. These are known as "Hoylake Medals" and the words have become associated with the actual trophies, although two of them are Cups and one a Claret Jug. For this reason I have chosen as a title for this chapter the words "The Hoylake Medals."

It is naturally the ambition of every good golfer to win one of these scratch prizes, and the title "Scratch Medallist at Hoylake," has some real significance. Mr. Horace Hutchinson in his book *Fifty Years of Golf*, records his pleasure at winning medals at Hoylake, especially during his year of captaincy. Before the war, the triumvirate, John Ball, Harold Hilton and Jack Graham, made it desperately hard for any other player to win, and the golfer who departed with one of these mementos in his pocket had every reason to be proud of himself.

THE CLUB GOLD MEDAL

A gold medal with the Club Crest, in enamel, in the centre, surrounded by a rose and thistle design; on the edge the words *Liverpool Golf Club*, 1869; the word *Royal* and the gold crown which surmounts the whole medal, were added later.

The history of the Club Gold Medal goes back to 1870, when at a meeting of the council, Mr. J. Muir Dowie, the first captain, suggested "that some consideration should be given to providing a gold medal for the Spring Meeting." It was purchased by a subscription of the members, at a cost of £70, and was first played for at the Spring Meeting of 1870. An account written at the time describes the weather conditions as being very bad—drenching rain and a strong wind. The

course had to be played twice, as it was then only nine holes; the medal was won by Mr. John Dun, "the father" of Hoylake golf, with a score of 96.

"The crack player of the club, Mr. John Dun, of Warrington, went out next .... after some beautiful play Mr. Dun got round in 96 strokes. The first round he played indifferently, and took 52, but in the second round, he did the remarkably good score of 44"

was a report of the golf in a local paper. Mr. Dun was then "declared" the winner.

John Dun — the first winner

THE DUN CHALLENGE CROSS

A silver Maltese cross, in the centre of which is a gold medallion of the Royal Liverpool Golf Club.

The Dun Challenge Cross was presented to the Club in 1873 by Mr. John Dun of Warrington who had been elected captain for that year. At once he proceeded to win his own cross with a score of 93, Mr. H.M. Buskin, a London golfer having beaten him by one stroke for the first scratch medal. The next ten years saw the names of many distinguished golfers engraved on this trophy, amongst them being Dr. Argyll Robertson, Mr. A. Stuart, and Mr. Gilbert Mitchell Innes, from Edinburgh, and Mr. Arthur Molesworth from Westward Ho.

H.R.H. THE DUKE OF CONNAUGHT'S CHALLENGE STAR

A silver star, with the Club Crest in gold in the centre, flanked by a thistle and rose, with a background of enamel, surrounded by the words *Royal Liverpool Golf Club* in gold on a silver ring. The whole star surmounted by a ducal crown, in gold and enamel.

In the year 1872, H.R.H. The Duke of Connaught became the President of the Club, and presented a silver challenge star as a scratch trophy, to be played for on the second day of the Spring Meeting.

The Duke of Connaught's Star

It was first played for in 1873, and was won by Mr. H.M.P. Buskin, of Blackheath, with a score of 88. A writer describes this round as being "the best performance yet achieved on the links."

LORD STANLEY OF ALDERLEY'S MEDAL

A gold medal with the words *Royal Liverpool Golf Club* round the edge. A medallion in the centre with the figure of a golfer, surmounted by a Liver and crossed golf-clubs, and backed by a cross and an oak leaf design; nine golf balls surround the edge of the medal.

It was first played for at the Spring Meeting of 1882, and was won by Mr. A.H. Molesworth, with a score of 86. The next year, Mr. E.J.B. Farrar, the author's father, won with a score of 90, and forty-four years later, in 1927, the author was himself successful. From 1886 to 1888, Mr J.E. Laidlay was the holder, his last win being in the remarkably high score of 95.

THE SINCLAIR CUP

A silver gilt two-handled cup with a cover, standing about fifteen inches high.

In 1910 Mr. A. Sinclair presented this cup to celebrate Mr. John Ball's seventh win in the Amateur Championship. It is played for at the Queen Victoria Commemoration Meeting held each year in June. The first winner was Mr. F.W.H. Weaver, the winning score being 77.

This is the last scratch medal presented to the Club, and although it is to honour Mr. John Ball, it is the only one that does not bear his name, perhaps he felt some diffidence about winning it.

THE LUBBOCK GOLD MEDAL

A circular gold medal, with a medallion in the centre surrounded by a wreath.

This medal was presented by Mr. John Dun in 1872, to be played for each year on August Bank Holiday. It is called "The Lubbock" medal in honour of the founder of that holiday. A report of the first meeting describes the depressing weather conditions: "A strong cold wind blew over the links, and in the afternoon rain fell heavily. The devotion of some members of the Club for golf, however, is equal to

anything, and many played on through the rain."
The medal was won by Mr. J.C. Baldwin, a London scratch golfer, with a score of 93.

THE DOWIE SILVER CUP

A silver cylindrical cup, six and a half inches high, with two handles, resting on four ball feet.

This cup was the first prize ever presented to the Club — the gift of the first captain, Mr. J. Muir Dowie. Originally to become the property of anyone winning it twice, these conditions were afterwards altered, making it into a perpetual Challenge Cup. Played for in the autumn of 1869, at the first meeting ever held by the Club, it was won by Mr. John Dun with a score of 103. "It was their first competitive meeting at which prizes were spiritedly offered, and energetically competed for ... After the wholesome and exhilarating labours of that breezy day, at six o'clock the members of the Club sat down at the Royal Hotel to a welcome and capital dinner."

Dowie Cup — the first trophy

THE HALL BLYTH GOLD MEDAL

An oblong gold medal with crossed clubs in the centre, and the words *Royal Liverpool Golf Club* round the edge. Above the medal a Liver with a crown and the Club motto.

First played at the Autumn Meeting of 1882, it was tied for by Mr. A.F. Macfie and Mr. A.H. Molesworth; Mr. Macfie won the tie and became the first holder; his score was 87.

THE KENNARD GOLD MEDAL

A medal in gold and enamel, in the centre a Liver, with crossed clubs, and a rose and thistle; surrounded by the words *Royal Liverpool Golf Club*, 1871. A crown and the Club motto, *"Far and Sure,"* surmount the medal.

Lieut-Colonel E.H. Kennard, the donor of the medal, was captain of the Club in 1871 and 1872; he was also associated with the Blackheath Club, holding the office of Field Marshal for many years. On the first two occasions the medal was won by Mr. H.M.P. Buskin.

The Kennard Gold Medal

THE STEWART-GOVANE CUP

A silver claret jug about thirteen inches high; on the lid a grape and vine leaf design.

Mr. Alexander Stewart, the captain in 1888, was the donor of this cup, first played for at the Autumn Meeting of that year, Mr. R.W. Brown being the winner.

THE MILLIGAN ST. ANDREW'S GOLD CROSS

A gold St. Andrew's cross; in the centre, a Liver, the motto, and crossed clubs, the whole device encircled with a gold crown; a gold leaf is fastened on the back to carry the names of the winners.

This beautiful medal was presented to the Club by Mr. Wyndham C.A. Milligan, the captain for the year 1875; it was first played for in December of that year, Mr. John F. Raimes winning with a score of 100. Mr. Tweedie, the Hon. Secretary, wrote in the records, "the weather was very boisterous," so this fact may have accounted for the high scoring.

This competition is held late in the year, so the winning scores are higher than at the other meetings. Mr. Ball has won this medal more often than any other — he has been successful on nineteen occasions!

(from *The Royal Liverpool Golf Club* published by Willmer Brothers 1933)

More about the Medals

John Behrend

Guy Farrar has described "The Hoylake Medals", telling us how and when they came to be presented. That was written in the 1930s, and since then two further Scratch trophies have been added. Gus Lowe, Captain in 1964, initiated a Club championship to be played over 36 holes at the end of each season. Tony Meyer, who had been an England boy international a few years earlier, was the first winner. The Club Champion receives a large gilt medallion — as awarded to the winners of the Club Gold Medal. In 1979 Michael Roberts had the idea that a competition should be played from the Championship tees, and presented a Cup for the best net score. A year later Michael had died, and the Bobby Jones Putter, a reproduction of "Calamity Jane" — the famous putter used in his Grand Slam year 50 years earlier — was presented as the Scratch trophy. It is mounted on a wooden base with a plaque to commemorate Michael, on which the names of the winners are also inscribed. Thus there are thirteen Scratch trophies played for each year, with nine gilt and four silver mementoes to be won.

Since the Club was formed, more than 1,000 Scratch medals have been awarded, and a couple of hundred members have had one or more of the replica medallions to show for it. One or more! — a great many more in the case of John Ball junior and Harold Hilton. John Ball joined the Club in October 1881 and within two days he had won his first Medal. He went on winning them with great regularity for 42 years — 113 in all (94 gold and 19 silver). Hilton in the twenty years from 1889 amassed a collection of 59 (35 gold and 24 silver). That still leaves a lot for distribution amongst the more ordinary mortals who have the added thrill of finding their name below that of an Open champion.

To Hilton fell the honour of achieving what must surely be the finest round in a Hoylake Medal competition. In 1900, with a gutty ball and hickory shafts, wearing, no doubt, a stiff collar and Norfolk jacket, he holed the course in 72 to win the Duke of Connaught's Star and break the record established the previous day (a 75 by Jack Graham) by three clear shots. It would have been by a greater margin but for a 6 at the final hole. More than 30 years elapsed before that score was beaten, Norman Fogg winning the Club Gold medal of 1933 with a 71.

In 1949 Ronnie White, Britain's leading Amateur at the time, achieved a magnificent 68 in the Autumn Meeting and although that score has been equalled in Club medals by Ian Bradshaw in 1979 and Steve Roberts in the 1981 Club championship it has not been beaten. In Steve's case his 68 followed scores of 69 and 72 in the previous two Medal competitions — surely the sharpest shooting ever achieved in one month. Rob Fitzpatrick and Stuart Danchin are the only other players to have broken the 70 barrier in one of the major Club Medals. However, with the proliferation of weekday competitions, there have been a number of other sub-70 scores, pride of place going to Graham Brown for his 66 in 1984 which stands as the Club Amateur record. He knew after 13 holes that he had the chance of a good score, but there were the five long and testing holes to face. Anyone who can keep his nerve and play them in two under fours, as Graham did, deserves to hold the record.

Graham Brown — amateur record holder

In 1887 John Ball won all six gold medals. What is perhaps more remarkable is that from August 1886 to May 1889 he won seventeen out of eighteen, missing only the Club Gold Medal at the 1888 Spring Meeting's first day. He had to content himself with the Dun Challenge Cross and silver memento. Again in 1892, 1906 and 1908 he won five of the six major awards. Michael Pearson is the only other Club member to have won six medals — 5 gold and 1 silver — in one year (1953); Ronnie White also won five gold medals in 1955. More recently Blyth Bell, in his first full year as a member of the Club, won five in a row (four gold and one silver) starting with the Sinclair Cup at the Queen Victoria Meeting of 1987.

Who is the youngest Medal winner and who is the oldest? For a change it is not John Ball. He was 19 when he joined the Club, but from the mid-1970s junior members of suitable standard were permitted to compete for the Scratch medals (but not the Handicap prizes) and both Mark and Andrew Jordan won gold medals as 16-year-olds. Neil McBurney and Ian Farrall were others to achieve this distinction as Juniors.

As for the oldest, Clifford Harrison, a fine golfer but better known as an international hockey player, had won a number of silver medals before the war, but never a gold one. He holed the course in 76 at the St. Andrew's Meeting of 1957 and was celebrating in a manner appropriate to a Gold medal and Sweep winner long before he was weighed in. Clifford was in his mid-60s at the time, and there have been few more popular wins.

Strangest story is of David Brown in the 1930s visiting his dentist and being told that a crown would be required for a broken tooth. An appointment was made for the following week. David duly arrived, and the dentist was somewhat startled by his request. "Use this", he said, and handed over the gold medal he had won at the weekend.

The most spectacular finish belongs to Ian Hudson, now resident in the Channel Islands. In the 1962 St. Andrew's Meeting he sank a 4-iron second shot at the 17th and holed for a 3 at the 18th; two pars for a respectable 77 had suddenly been converted into a Medal-winning 74.

John Graham remembers playing at the end of the field in the 1946 Summer Meeting on a day when a strong wind strengthened to gale force. He was greeted by Guy Farrar as he came off the 18th green. "How have you done?" asked Guy. "No good — I'm going to tear it up" came the reply. Farrar encouraged him to sign the card and hand it over. He glanced at it and announced "You've tied for the Gold Medal"; the score was an 86. John's opponent in the play-off had no pretensions of winning a Scratch prize, and failed to break 100, thus leaving John with the doubtful honour of the highest Gold Medal winning score since the demise of the gutty ball. Jim McBurney junior matched it winning the 1976 Dowie Cup. One suspects that the weather may have been unfavourable on that occasion too!

There have been many stories of misfortune, but here are two recent ones, the first with a happy ending. Nick Beggs, one of the Club colts, produced a brilliant 73 in the 1988 Summer Meeting to scoop the pool, Gold Medal and Handicap prize, as he thought. Unfortunately his card added up to 72. In his excitement he had failed to check the individual scores at each hole, and was disqualified. Nick shrugged off his disappointment with a rueful smile, and next time, in the first day of the Autumn Meeting, turned in a 75 (checked and found correct) and duly won the Dowie Cup and his first Gold Medal — another popular winner. In the 1989 Club Championship, Rob Fitzpatrick completed the afternoon round in 68 to add, so he believed, to a morning round of 74 giving him a total one shot less than Stuart Danchin and Blyth Bell. On returning to the Clubhouse he found that he had not signed his morning card and had therefore been disqualified. Danchin's superb 1-iron at the first play-off hole earned him the title, and Rob will have to wait to win his second Club championship (he won in 1986). It won't be long for sure.

Hard-luck stories are the bread and butter of Hoylake Medals. "I was going well until I hit two out of bounds at the 16th" . . . "Just fell into the bunker with my second shot and thinned it on to the road" . . ."Something should be done about the face of that bunker on the 18th". We've heard it all before, and in truth we don't listen any more — unless we are in with a 74, and there's nothing better, and the last pair with a chance of beating it are playing the 18th. A few minutes later they are in the Clubhouse with their own disappointments to recount, "Oh what bad luck" you say, and the moment of exhilaration has arrived when you realise you've won the Gold Medal.

The Wind of Change

John Graham

I started playing golf as a lad at Hoylake nearly 70 years ago in the very early 1920s during the Charleston and Flapper era. Since then, not surprisingly, there have been a considerable number of changes. Every hole has been altered in some major or minor way. The perimeter of the practice field used to be guarded by a continuous bunker down the first and sixteenth fairways. This prevented one's ball from trickling out-of-bounds, albeit at the expense of a bunker shot. Out-of-bounds cost distance only and stymies were legal.

I suppose the biggest change has been in the habits of the Club. In my early days Liverpool was an affluent and important city revolving around shipping, cotton broking and ancillary services such as banking, insurance, law, accountancy, etc. Fortunes were made and lost frequently. Throughout the Club there was considerable wealth. Nearly everyone had servants. The large majority of the younger members had been to public schools. We had a very healthy respect for the senior members. We called them "Sir" whenever they spoke to us. It was not advisable to upset them. Richard Cornelius recounts the occasion when he became a member in 1931. He ventured, for the first time, into the Clubroom. Sitting in an armchair was an elderly and rather small member who turned round and said "What are you doing here, boy? Out!" It was two years before Richard ventured into that room again. Business was not supposed to be discussed in the Clubhouse. Indeed I remember the occasion when a high official of a well-known service company was blackballed because it was feared that he would try to get business from the members if he joined.

Until the late 1950s the ladies were definitely taboo and were second-class citizens. It was a man's Club. There was the occasion, my father told me, when a long suffering wife wanted to get her errant husband back home and looked through the bar window in the front of the Clubhouse (where it was in those days) to see if he was there. On her tiptoes she saw him and banged on the window to catch his attention. This so outraged the members that it was decided to raise the window one foot higher so that no lady could ever look in again. Within a week this was done.

Plus-fours, alas, have gone. The ladies, who now play at will around the links, wear trousers and knickerbockers. What would the late lamented Guy Farrar have said! I have been through the whole gamut of the female saga — from the period of taboo, through the thin end of the wedge period, to the present day and, in order not to be completely ostracised by the opposite sex, may I hasten to say what a charming change it has been.

Between the Wars there was always a number of members playing in the various Championships both at home and abroad. And we had some successes. Froes Ellison (twice winner of the English Close Championship), Eustace Landale and Allan Graham (both finalists in the Amateur) and Bruce Thompson (winner of the Belgian Championship) are some of them. Alas, today it is rare to see a member of the Club playing in any of them. A number of us, besides playing in the Home Championships, used to play in the Continental Championships and what fun they were. The golf was good and the courses excellent and we used to get through the odd round or so.

Members took a much greater interest in their fellow-members' golf than they do today. The Captain's Prize final would have a following of at least 50 people. In a Colt's match, the top pair would draw 50–75 people, and more would watch Club matches. On the odd occasion, when I won a competition, I always received half-a-dozen letters of congratulations from some of the more senior members. It was tremendously encouraging.

Those inter-war years were the last period of "gracious living". Dinner was served in the Club each night. Gin was about 37½ pence a bottle when I became a member in 1933. Although there were strict rules regarding behaviour, etiquette and dress (I was once turned off the Links by Forbes Bell, the Secretary, for wearing a bright green shirt), there was a certain laxity over the hours. One could nearly always get a drink in the Steward's room upstairs. Many a time I have played poker in the Club till 2 or 3 am. The staff did not mind. We always put 10 per cent of every reasonable win in a pot for them and in no time it became a small fortune. The staff, therefore, had a vested interest in our game, and would gladly make us eggs and bacon at midnight if we wished.

There were big changes in golf equipment. Until 1931 or 1932, I played with wooden-shafted clubs and had amassed by then a driver, brassie, spoon, mid-iron, jigger, mashie, mashie-niblick and putter. They were beautiful clubs and I assiduously looked after them. After every day's play, I cleaned the irons with emery paper and chains. It was sheer joy to go into the professional's shop and see the Youds family, wearing their craftsmen's aprons, filing a wooden head down to exact specification. Then came the Big Bang — the advent of the steel-shafted golf club. Hoylake "cottoned on" fairly quickly and in next to no time we were all using them! In the early 1930s there were two types of steel shaft at Hoylake — the True Temper, which was whippy and looked like a telescopic fishing rod, and the Apollo which was a rather stiff shaft. I settled for the Apollo, but most of my friends used the True Temper.

The golf ball has not changed all that much. When I was a lusty youth before the War, I had reached every long hole with a drive and a No. 8 iron. I doubt if the golf ball goes all that much further today. A Silver King used to be my favourite ball, although a Dunlop took over towards the second half of the 1930s.

Ever since the Club began in 1869, singing has been a feature after Club dinners, especially after the St. Andrew's Dinner. The piano was always there and many songs were sung with great gusto. If you wished to play billiards, snooker, bridge or merely drink, you did just that. But many of us would let our hair down with the "Men of Harlech", the "Ball of Kirriemuir" or the latest rugger ballad of the time. For some unknown reason the custom was discontinued a few years after the Second World War. Please can we start it up again? After all the piano, a little battered, is still there.

Hoylake at War

Gordon Williamson

ANTICIPATION AND PREPARATION

The drums rolled and the sirens wailed but the British people did not! The long expected happened and, quite gradually at first, the momentous change from peacetime routine and habits took place. During the last days of August and early September 1939 it was a very different matter for the regular, territorial and volunteer forces; for them it was all go from the start.

The Club Officials — Captain Otho Glover, Treasurer Alan Chambers, Secretary H.C. Forbes Bell with the support of the Council members — had to face early on the reduction of income because of the absence of and loss of subscriptions from serving members. Recently formed local units such as 149 Regt., R.H.A. in Hoylake and 93rd Regt., A.A. in Wirral had attracted a good number of members during the previous year's recruitment. Facilities in the Club House were made available; for instance, bathrooms for the local Searchlight Detachment between 7 and 9.30 am, and temporary house membership for the Officers Mess of the 149 Regt., "The Hoylake Horse". All on the basis that a clean and happy soldier goes to make a good soldier!

To instance a few of the many efforts to economise or improve the depleted income ... the Council decided to have 100 sheep grazing on the hallowed course ... a rent of £4 per annum to be charged for ground used by the Searchlight Detachment ... The Club House to close at 8pm ... No dinners to be served and, lastly, no toast to be served at tea time!

REALITY 10TH MAY 1940

The shattering clap of thunder ended the illusory calm of the "phoney war" when, after eight months of static positions in Western Europe, the Blitzkrieg erupted after the fall of Denmark and Norway during the preceding April. On the 14th May the appeal for volunteers for a citizens' Army was broadcast on the radio. Thus was initiated the start of the Local Defence Volunteers (L.D.V.) which subsequently and rightly became the Home Guard, and so was raised the 17th Bn. Cheshire Regt. (Home Guard). Hoylake's contribution was No. 2 Platoon A Company. Originally they called themselves "The Green Lodge Crowd", a suitable establishment for concentration! Wearing arm bands and civvies, while carrying such cudgels with which they could arm themselves, they paraded under the majestic presence and command of Dan Toby supported by the strong arm of Clifford Harrison. All sizes and shapes were represented by such as Harold (Woolly) Jager, Matt White, Arthur Sainsbury, Puff Cornelius and, not least, Johnnie Beavan. After the Evacuation at Dunkirk and by August 1940 the platoon was issued with denims and rifles, at first with the Ross and then the

Inspection in the Field — "by the left", Arnet Robinson and Matt White

Springfield as well as two Browning Automatics. Being now uniformed, the experience of World War I was evident by the medal ribbons worn. The Battalion Commander held the D.S.O., and there were four M.C.S and one D.S.M.

It is salutory to remember the immense efforts and the spirit displayed by such volunteers who trained for home defence, patrolled at night, worked at the jobs by day and suffered grievous loss of business and property during the increasing air raids upon Merseyside. Altogether during hostilities about 320 were enrolled and passed through No. 2 Platoon. Many were engaged eventually in the regular forces, of whom 5 were killed or missing.

On a lighter note, as with many another unit, mishaps and strange events occurred. Rounds inadvertently discharged upon the order "Ease Springs"PIAT rounds fired supposedly in practice but in the event "live" with surprising results. There was the reported encounter of Roland (Rusty) Marshall with top brass at his home at the far end of the course, where a high-level "recce" took place to site pill boxes, minefield and wire. The owner was astonished to hear upon his return home from Liverpool one evening that the field of fire was obstructed by his substantial house and that it had to be demolished! It is believed that the owner's outburst in legal measured terms was such that the brilliant idea was scotched! During September 1940 the countrywide stand to, invasion imminent (codenamed "Cromwell") was signalled and so the platoon manned their allotted road blocks all night. A local military unit offered them bacon butties but one member was denied such refreshment due to the rapidity with which he responded to the call out. He had forgotten his teeth.

THE CLUB'S HOLDING OPERATION

Faith, hope, and not a little charity were needed to keep the club ticking over, however quietly, during the dark days of the early years. Due to call up under conscription many changes in staff took place, with male staff replaced by waitresses. Meals and bar facilities became more and more meagre. The few meetings of the House Committee recorded all this but the major problem, arising when they did meet, concerned the rapid diminution of supplies of gin and whisky. Imagine the effect on certain members when told that only one bottle of gin could be put out during each day, with the bonus of two on Saturdays and Sundays. For the inner man and the Club House, fuel became scarcer and scarcer. Despite considerable influence in certain quarters, even vintage port became a luxury!

Although some stalwarts together with a few service personnel on leave were able to keep the game of golf alive, the course suffered the experiences of service as much as the members. Sleepers and posts were erected to prevent the landing of enemy planes and/or gliders. From the 9th tee to the 12th green along the line of the dunes, barbwire entaglements enclosed an extensive minefield. In the area of the Black Steps, pill boxes were built. At one time representations had to be made that the farmer was grazing far more sheep than originally permitted. You can imagine just what an effect this enlarged flock had upon the bunkers! Various local rules were adopted to accommodate these hazards including that which stipulated that a golf ball played into the minefield might be dropped without penalty on the fairway. It is not recorded how many were retrieved! Even the searchlight detachment was not out of the line of fire as the ball had to be played where it lay unless the shot was obstructed.

During these years the Club suffered the news of the death of John Ball in December 1940 and in July 1941 that of Allan Graham after 40 years of membership. History records that their exploits were truly heroic. Another major blow was the death of the Secretary Major H.C. Forbes Bell in July 1944. He had held the post since 1923. As a result Guy Farrar was appointed just at a time when his knowledge of course management was so important to bring Hoylake back to its pre-war condition. Finally in this roll of honour it has to be recorded that our President H.R.H. The Duke of Connaught died in 1942 having served in that capacity for over 70 years — since 1871 just two years after the founding of the Club! Subsequently, of course, the Club was honoured by the agreement of H.R.H. Prince Philip, The Duke of Edinburgh, to be Patron of the Club.

THE SCENT OF VICTORY

After the successful landings in Normandy and in time the rapid advance across France and Belgium, the pulse of activity quickened through the Club and its "guardian members". There was much to be done on the course even though that part of it, which had been available for play, was in fair order through the comparative reduction of play during the war years. Guy Farrar was subsequently asked how it was that the greens on the seaward side of the course were brought back into play so quickly and in such good order. The reason was simplicity itself though perhaps reprehensible. By a covert arrangement with the soldiery doing the wiring job in 1940, access through the wire had been made to allow a mower to be moved on to the respective greens and thus they were regularly cut.

Obstructions such as the minefield, pill boxes and wire were yet to be dealt with, and Sappers were not available to clear the mines. The War Office wanted to stop paying rent for the land requisitioned, but this was rejected by the Council until the land was cleared for golf or for extended grazing by sheep — not that their presence would have been welcomed a moment longer, but it was a good excuse! Members who had so carefully taken charge of the Club Silver and Trophies were relieved of their responsibility and the various items returned to the Club House.

Eventually after V.E. day the minefield was cleared, contractors were employed to remove the wire and demolish the pill boxes. The sheep at long last had their final bite at the fairways and so a start was made to repair the bunkers on the first six holes. Forward planning was the order of the day. Estimates of likely expense to be incurred on the course and Club House were calculated within the limits of likely income and the continued restrictions of war-time conditions.

Some of us may still be old enough to remember that splendid *Punch* cartoon by Bruce Bairnsfather depicting Old Bill squatting in a flooded shell hole saying to his mate "If you know of a better 'ole, go to it!" For those returning home and even those still in the Far East the Club indeed was a better 'ole even if all eighteen holes were not yet in prime condition.

Sadly it is recorded upon the World War II memorial in the Club Room the names of fifteen members who did not return "Home from the Hill" to rejoin those who did. However, for those many who did survive it was a case of "Far and Sure" — the Club's motto — and the knowledge of a successful job well done.

The Professionals

Leslie Edwards

In the course of its long history the Royal Liverpool Club has been served by a small, but distinguished, band of professionals. It is appropriate, I think, that they should be named in the order in which they appeared and that tribute should be paid them in any anthology. They were: Jack Morris, Jack Youds, Jimmy Adams, Cyril Hughes, Campbell Adamson, John Morgan and John Heggarty.

Morris had his shop (if shop it could be called in 1869) in the stabling behind the Royal Hotel in Stanley Road. The billiard room of this famous three-storeyed brick-built building (used initially by the Lord Stanley of that day as a place in which he could spend summer holidays and bathe in the sea) had become the headquarters of the newly formed Liverpool Golf Club, the opening hole of which later became the eighteenth.

Jack Morris

I have heard it said authoritatively that after his first fortnight at Hoylake, Morris felt so homesick he wrote to his father telling him that he was determined to return home. The response to this was sage advice to stay on awhile and to see whether he liked the job any better. He did. He stayed on for 60 eventful years, retiring when his Club had marked his magnificent service by making him an honorary life member.

Professionals at Hoylake have had three different work places. When the present Clubhouse was built Morris's shop was the first floor room, which is now the ladies' lounge. When Jack Youds, a local man, joined Morris in partnership in 1909 he asked the Club Council if the Club would build them a new shop at ground level. This lead to the professional's shop being moved to its present location at the further end of the Clubhouse, near where members now leave the Clubhouse from the locker rooms.

Morris and Youds, as a team and as individuals, satisfied fully the requirements of a host of marvellous championship players, among them John Ball, Harold Hilton and Jack Graham. However all was not perfect harmony as the Club Minutes of long ago reveal.

For example:
8 Feby, 1910: A long discussion ensued on the question of Morris and Youds, Mr. Dun explaining the position and stating that on terms which he gave, Youds proposed to buy Morris out subject to the Council granting him the shop on the same terms as Morris had always enjoyed.

1 March, 1910: On the question of Morris and Youds in the absence of Mr. Dun the secretary stated that he understood Youds would not accept an annual tenancy and that they had decided to go on with the old partnership arrangement.

6 Sept, 1910: The secretary reported that Morris and Youds had dissolved partnership, the latter having bought Morris out subject to the Council giving Youds a tenancy of the shop.

The bare bones of Morris's career are illuminating. He was born at St. Andrews in 1847 and died in Hoylake in November, 1929. Old Tom Morris was his uncle and Young Tom his cousin. To illustrate the long service of Morris at Hoylake Young Tommy was holding the first of his four Open titles in the year his cousin took up his appointment here. He frequently acted as starter at Open and Amateur championships at Hoylake. I found him a somewhat forbidding character. His trousers, usually of tweed, were always immaculately pressed and his black brogue shoes bore a shine worthy of any sergeant in The Guards. He almost invariably wore a peaked yachting cap. His command to a player on the first tee, unlike the absurd ritual which happens so often to-day, was "Play away, sir!"

The finest, most affectionate, tribute to Morris is contained in the legendary Bernard Darwin's book, *Life Is Sweet, Brother*. He wrote:

> The first time I ever played in the Amateur Championship, at Hoylake in 1898, I met another Scottish professional of a very different type, Jack Morris, a nephew of Old Tom's, and one of the most entirely charming old gentlemen that ever lived. Old Tom, to my sorrow, I hardly knew, and so the only comparison I can make is with old Charley Hunter of Prestwick. It would be impossible to think of two men of more natural good breeding and more perfect manners. Jack had come to Hoylake as little more than a boy when the club was first founded in 1869. It was a bleak spot — a rabbit warren, a race-

course and the then solitary bulk of the Royal Hotel. His father brought him there and, deeming the prospect too dreary for the boy, said that there seemed to be little doing and that, if he liked, he might pack up and return to Scotland. The boy, however, decided to stick it out, and he stayed there till at the end of his long life he took his ease as an honorary member of the club. That was the time to sidle up to him, when he was reading a newspaper in the club-house over a cigar, and extract memories from him. I have forgotten too many of them, but I remember very well his talking of Allan Robertson. "Once he gave me a sixpence. That was a lot of money for a poor boy in those days." One of the last occasions on which I saw him was on a day of blazing sunshine, when he kindly walked me all the way across the course to show me the site, now overgrown with bents, of the old Meols green. When we came back, and indeed on many other occasions, he privily slipped a cigar into my coat pocket "because," he explained, "my daughter says you write nice things about me in the papers." It was and is quite impossible to write them nicely enough.

As a personal refection on this delightful story I would add that in 60 years of writing on golf and other sports I wrote thousands of nice things about hundreds of those I counted as heroes. Only three of them — Lord Mildmay, Gladys Temple Dobell and Frances Smith — were ever kind enough to acknowledge my references to them, much less privily slip a cigar into my coat pocket!

Jimmy Adams

James Adams, whose spell at Hoylake followed that of the Morris—Youds era, was a tournament player fated to wear the awful label carried by a man who nearly always came second. Indeed in his later playing days he was frequently referred to as James the Second. He bore the indignity with characteristic phlegm and good humour. It had no effect on him or his golf. It was a soubriquet undeserved because he did win major events, but never the Open championship or the professional match-play championship.

Champion or not, his record in professional golf was remarkable: second in two Opens within three years; losing finalist in three match-play championships; fourth at Portrush in Max Faulkner's Open and third to Peter Thomson in the Open of 1954. Until 1950 he was also a stalwart of the British Ryder Cup team.

He had finished runner-up to Alf Padgham in the memorable Open at Hoylake in 1936 before joining the Royal Liverpool Club as professional. He finished second in the 1938 Open at Sandwich where, in hurricane conditions, he fought a day-long duel with the winner, Reggie Whitcombe, with whom he had been paired for the final 36 holes of that momentous day. Had the Open been played now in a gale of similar severity play would be abandoned. Whitcombe twice needed four putts. The larger-size American ball, now in general use, would inevitably have been blown, continually, from every green. Adams was such a delightful friend of mine, I went with him to Renshaw Hall in Liverpool when he joined the R.A.F.

Adams learned his golf at Troon. He was a burly chap with a ruddy complexion, a slight speech impediment, and almost the sailor's rolling gait. It was impossible not to like him. His sense of humour was sharp; his backswing so pronouncedly long any video shot of him must have shown the head of the club in the vicinity of his left heel! Yet what a fine player he was and notably when he fought for his side against the Americans. One of his assistants at Hoylake during his comparatively short stay at Hoylake was little Hugh Watt, later a renowned professional at Gullane and one, unhappily, who was to enjoy only a few days of retirement.

After leaving Hoylake Adams spent many years with the Royal Mid-Surrey club where after his retirement at 66 he played frequently. He told me not long before he died: "I was never a good enough player to win championships, but ironically after I'd retired I played better than I had ever played before."

With Adams in 1940 serving in the R.A.F. and the links in war-time order with mines and anti-invasion trenches causing occasional embarrassment to the few members who were able to play, golf at Hoylake was confined to the aged and some of the Royal Navy top brass operating from the Western Approaches headquarters in Liverpool. The needs of members at that time were catered for by Youds, who not long afterwards ended his long association with the Club, mostly as a clubmaker. And what a craftsman clubmaker!

It was in 1940 that the Club decided to appoint another professional to succeed Adams. They chose a Hoylake man, Cyril Hughes, who had returned in 1933 after a successful career in American golf. He had a number of connections with the Club. He was a godson of Hoylake's most famous figure John Ball, who was also his second cousin, and his uncle Herbert had been caddie-master for a while.

Cyril had learned his golf at Hoylake before being appointed professional to the Chester Club, where many Hoylake members played Sunday golf before the ban on Sunday play was belatedly lifted at their own course. Like Charles Ward, Hughes had, for a top-class tournament golfer, an unusual build. He was not

Cyril Hughes with Walter Hagen

many inches taller than five feet and walked with a slight limp. Neither of these physical disadvantages weighed with him. In a golfing sense he had the heart of a lion. This he proved when, as a young man starting out in the game, he surprised everyone by reaching the semi-finals of the match-play championship at Sunningdale and was beaten, if memory serves, by George Duncan. He played in the Open of 1912 at Muirfield, the Open of 1913, which J.H. Taylor won, at Hoylake, in one of the greatest gales ever to afflict the competition, the Open at Prestwick in 1914 and at Deal in 1920 where he finished down the list but only one stroke inferior to James Braid. In the same year he had won one of the oldest championships in professional golf, the Leeds Cup. He then left to join his father who had for some time been a golf professional in America.

Charles Elston, a distinguished member of the Club, had some remarkable recollections of Cyril Hughes and his golfing family. Cyril's uncle, a member of the Village Play Club, was one of the many fishermen who earned their living from local waters. He had a shrimp round — on foot! — and was well liked as a real Hoylake character. He was as proud of his nephew, especially when he did so well in American Opens, as he was of his brother. Cyril, like his father became an American citizen, but during his years in the United States, as his Club was closed by the wintry conditions for some months each year, he used to return for a holiday at Hoylake. In crossing the Atlantic more than twenty times he had to contend with some horrendous voyages. When he finally returned to Britain with his father in 1933 there was a seven year ban on him working here, and not only that ... he had to report every month for seven years at Hoylake police station. They lived in Airlie Road off Meols Drive so Charles Elston recalls.

Cyril's years at Royal Liverpool before retirement and the coming of Campbell Adamson to fill his place must have been among the happiest of his life. He was liked by everyone. The way he braced himself against the Hoylake gales and steered his shots low and accurately through the wind were the pattern of what good golf should be in difficult links conditions. His second marriage was to the daughter of Steve Beck, the Hoylake caddie master who lost a leg in the First World War and soldiered on to give splendid service to the club. Cyril and Mary had a son, photographed as a babe with Johnny Bulla on the practice green during the 1947 Open. The boy grew up to become a brilliant student. He married and then tragically died young from cancer.

Cyril Hughes was a superb golfer even in his fifties and sixties. His keenest fan at the club was David Brown, probably the most delightful eccentric the club ever enjoyed and at best a golfer who could give Cyril Tolley a testing match. David persisted in coming home from the office in the evening and insisting on taking Cyril out until dusk, if not moonlight. One evening when David was seen heading for the professional's shop one of Cyril's assistants warned: "Look out ... Here comes Mr. Brown to take you out!" Cyril doubled himself up and crouched into the knee-hole of his immense roll-top desk. David came in, and being told that Cyril had gone for tea, stayed half an hour chatting to the assistant. When he had left, Cyril emerged seized with cramp and moving like the moustachioed Marx brother.

In retirement Cyril lived in a lovely house at Pant, near Oswestry, and died in his nineties. At his home he had a garden with terraced lawns on several levels. From these he played chip shots from one to the other without harm to the carefully nurtured velvety turf.

Campbell Adamson was no less well liked than his predecessor. He proved to be precisely what the club had hoped for — a steady, reliable, cheerful servant, a good teacher and maker and repairer of crafted clubs. He played only occasionally in tournaments, but he did join John Graham in playing in the Centenary Open championship at St Andrews and again, with John, won the Spalding Cup

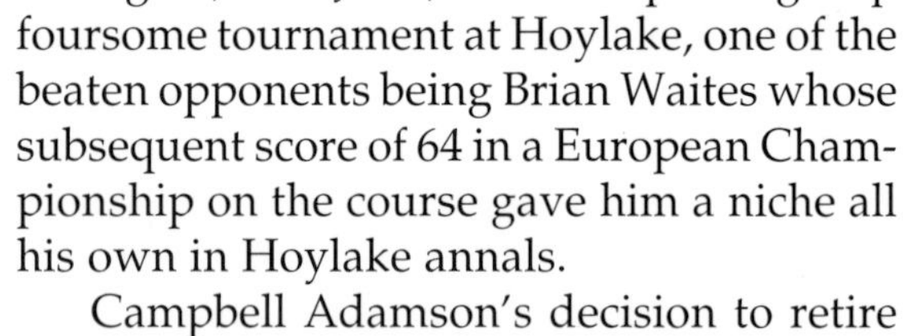

foursome tournament at Hoylake, one of the beaten opponents being Brian Waites whose subsequent score of 64 in a European Championship on the course gave him a niche all his own in Hoylake annals.

Jock Adamson

Campbell Adamson's decision to retire and to go and live in North Wales everyone regretted. And now, when one tries to get in touch with him by telephone, the message is invariably borrowed from the Bing Crosby refrain "Gorn fishin' "!

Adamson was followed by John Morgan, a Hoylake man and former Cheshire county player whose decision to turn professional came only after he had for some years worked as a Physical Education schoolteacher. He was formerly attached to the Stoneham club in Hampshire. Considering that he was in his mid-twenties when he relinquished his amateur status he has had remarkable success. An early attempt in an Open at Carnoustie ended somewhat disastrously in that he failed to qualify. But there were extenuating circumstances. In one round, in placing his hand behind his ball in the rough to test its lie, he was bitten through his golf glove by a rat and had to have the wound cauterised. Henry Longhurst, to whom I retailed this unusual event next morning, said "Fancy going back home and being asked how you fared. And all you could say was '81 and 84 and beaten by a rat!' "

But Morgan has since more than made up for his false start in that Open. Indeed, on one occasion, he led an illustrious Open field and on others he has figured prominently besides having won events on the European Tour and in Africa among top-class tournament playing professionals.

John Heggarty

Which brings me to the present and to John Heggarty, the young Scot from Dumfries who has proved himself an excellent teacher, a cheerful character in all circumstances and a golfer who, if he really wanted that kind of life, could more than hold his own among top tournament players. His wife, Helen, is the former Girl champion and former champion of Cheshire.

John may not aspire to matching Jack Morris's sixty years' service, but he has made a good start and one hopes it will be many more years before he decides to hang up his video camera.

It Happened at Hoylake

Nicko Williams

When John Graham appealed for anecdotes for this chapter in the autumn of 1989, there was only a modest response so that much of the material is modern. Nevertheless it is appropriate that the first tale concerns one of Hoylake's greatest figures, Harold Hilton.

Hilton, whilst in his prime, was challenged by the Artisans or Village Play as they are now known, to a rather special competition. The wager was £100 — a considerable sum in those days. The condition was that each player be confined to two clubs. The opponent was to select the player's club for every shot except the tee shot. Hilton accepted the challenge. Upon arrival at the first tee, his opponent, the Villagers' champion, asked which two clubs Hilton had chosen. Upon his reply that he was carrying two similar cleeks, the Villagers promptly submitted and lost the wager.

The members of Hoylake are probably typical of any golf club. With few exceptions they are genial, generous and not conspicuously well behaved. The following story could come from any age, but must have given the council of the time some ticklish moments.

During the 1930s a member of some standing (reputedly a retired Colonel) was discovered in his car in a compromising situation with a female member of the staff. The place in which they were found was just to the left of the seventh green.

At the ensuing Council meeting, it was pointed out that the Club had expectations of an inheritance from the gentleman concerned. This caused a degree of controversy, because one faction of the council was adamant that he should be expelled, but the remainder wished to be more pragmatic in the hope of retaining the inheritance for the Club.

Eventually a compromise was found; since the gentleman in question was "out of bounds" at the time, then the Club's rules did not apply.

When I joined the Club in the early 1960s it was full of wonderful eccentrics. "Basher" Hayes was a keen golfer and liked a few holes with the young, and he asked me to join him one Saturday morning. After three holes he rather curiously requested to play back to the clubhouse. Nonplussed and a little concerned, I accompanied Basher back to the locker room where another young member was waiting for him. After another three holes they both returned again. By lunchtime Basher had played 18 holes with six different partners.

Absent-minded Colonel Linsell was a lovely old fellow who inhabited the club room peering out over the course with the binoculars. One afternoon and for no obvious reason he "torpedoed" another motorist as he turned into Meols Drive from the club car park. The irate motorist demanded that the Colonel follow him to Hoylake police station to be charged with careless driving. The Colonel readily acceded and followed meekly behind. Unfortunately he failed to notice either the police station or that his protagonist had stopped outside it, and with another tremendous crash the Colonel repeated his earlier performance.

The car park, which until the late 1950s used to be a bowling green, has been the scene of one or two other incidents over the years.

An old lady in a scruffy raincoat was walking out of the car park to the bus stop when a new member stopped and asked: "Can I give you a lift?" As she got into his car, he added: "How long have you been working here?" "Oh, I'm a member" she replied. The new member became even more embarrassed when he discovered that she was a past lady captain and the sister of Hoylake's senior past captain.

During the 1960s and early 1970s, the club was served by two elderly and mildly eccentric stewards, Grimshaw and Read. Grimshaw was never quite in the right place at the right time and shouts of "Grimshaw" would echo through the clubhouse. My brother later named his black retriever Grimshaw because the call came so naturally.

Just prior to the Amateur Championship in 1962 the excellent and energetic secretary of the R & A, Brigadier Brickman, "Brick" to his friends, was accompanying the R & A Championship Committee on their final visit to the course before the championship commenced. The R & A delegation and the RLGC championship committee congregated in the council room, but of "Brick" there was no sign. The club captain summoned Grimshaw to order a round of drinks while they waited and when the steward returned the irate chairman looked at his watch and said: "Where the hell is that BF Brickman?" Overhearing this and showing a rare and in this case rather unfortunate display of initiative, Grimshaw ambled from room to room enquiring for — "Mr. B.F. Brickman please. Mr B.F. Brickman wanted by the captain, in the Council room." Those within earshot thoroughly enjoyed the explanation that a seriously disgruntled secretary of the R & A demanded.

Jock Warnock was captain in 1962 and Nobby Roberts in 1954. Jock is a genial and sharp-witted Scotsman from whom nothing escapes, whilst Nobby, rarely bested in banter, was an equally genial and alert Welshman whose eccentric bridge calls and doubtful putting alarmed his more conservative partners. They frequently played golf with Tony Dalziel and the tall, taciturn and immaculately mannered Claud Dundas. On the twelfth Nobby had a very short putt to halve the hole. He looked up at Claud inquisitively. Not a muscle moved. As soon as he'd jabbed it past the hole he rounded mildly, but firmly, on Claud. "Any gentleman would have given me that putt." "Ah yes, my dear Nobby", replied Claud, "but I'm not a gentleman, I am an aristocrat." Which was true.

John Barrett joined the club in the late 1960s having been captain of Royal Mid-Surrey and a games player of great distinction. He had a beautiful old-fashioned golf swing and a considerable thirst. He was known as the Duke of Angostura, or the Duke for short, because of his penchant for pink gins. He very rarely played before lunch which was always substantial and purely hydraulic. On one of the rare occasions he did play before midday, it was for the Club against Birkdale in the bottom foursome. His tough match went all the way and it was a very weary Duke who arrived rather late at the lunch table to find the RLGC captain, shuffling his team to retrieve the morning's play, had put him at the head of the afternoon's foursomes due out very shortly. Leaning back in his chair and puffing on a cigarette he was heard to say rather plaintively: "Playing in the morning is one thing, but never before have I been asked to play two rounds before lunch."

There have been many other good golfers at Hoylake who could only play after refreshment, including Clifford Harrison and David Brown. In 1953 they played together in a match for the Club against the Seniors. Clifford Harrison was a celebrated local games player before and after the Second World War and frequently played top couple with David Brown, another great Hoylake foursomes player, but they lost that morning by 7 and 5. They may or may not have shared John Barrett's views, but, as always with the Seniors match, there was plenty of time for lunch, and in the afternoon they beat the same opponents by 8 and 6.

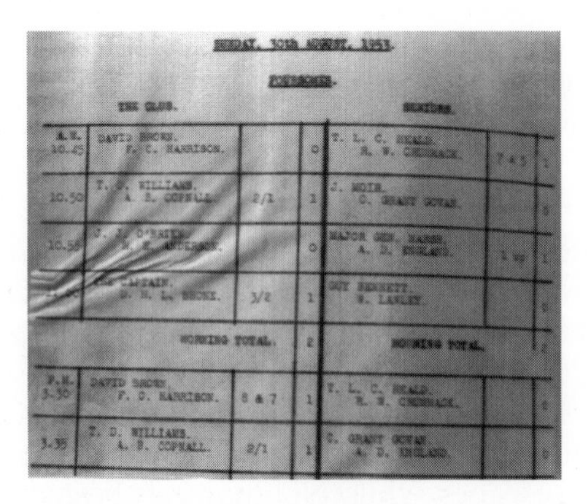

[illegible] 1953.

FOURSOMES.

THE CLUB.				SENIORS.		
A.M. 10.45	DAVID BROWN. F. C. HARRISON.		0	T. L. C. HEALD. [illegible]	7 & 5	1
10.50	T. [illegible] WILLIAMS. A. B. COPNALL.	2/1	1	J. MOIR. C. GRANT GOVAN.		0
[illegible]	[illegible]		0	MAJOR GEN. [illegible] A. D. [illegible]	1 up	1
[illegible]	THE CAPTAIN. [illegible]	3/2	1	GUY BENNETT. [illegible]		0
	MORNING TOTAL.		2	MORNING TOTAL.		2
P.M. 3.30	DAVID BROWN. F. C. HARRISON.	[illegible]	1	T. L. C. HEALD. [illegible]		0
3.35	T. D. WILLIAMS. A. B. COPNALL.	2/1	1	C. GRANT GOVAN. A. D. [illegible]		0

After-lunch golf

P.R.S. Williams was one of a very dangerous set of young men who were very much part of the Club scene during the 1960s and 1970s. His swing was stylish and everything looked right, but it must be said that he rarely troubled par. John Behrend, a county golfer and one of the best foursomes players in the country, took pity on him and invited him to play in the summer foursomes where they lost very comfortably in the first round. "I'm dreadfully sorry", apologised PRSW, "you could have counted my decent shots on the fingers of one hand." Quick as a flash and quite unmaliciously, John responded "More like Douglas Bader's toes, if I may say so." Incidentally it was at Hoylake that Bader with his artificial legs first broke 80, as witness the article in the downstairs bar.

Many of the great championships have already been chronicled, but there were other professional events held at Hoylake, including the *News of the World* Matchplay Championship in September 1956. Tony Colvin refereed one game and remembers it well. "I refereed a match between J.A. Jacobs of Lindrick, no relation to the renowned golf tutor, and F.S. Boobyer of Highgate. It was a closely contested match and on the 17th tee Jacobs was one up. After two good drives down the fairway, Jacobs played first and put his second into the heart of the green. Boobyer followed him with an equally good shot but as his ball dropped there was a gasp of consternation from the gallery thronging the green. When we reached the green it transpired that Boobyer's ball had unbelievably landed full pitch on top of Jacobs' ball. The result was that Jacobs' ball had shot hard left into a greenside bunker whereas Boobyer's ball had been diverted to the right and had ended out of bounds in Stanley Road. What an extraordinary incident and naturally I, as referee, was asked for a ruling. My opinion was that Jacobs could replace his ball without penalty on the green, but Boobyer was out of bounds, and would have to play another ball under normal penalty provisions. Both players accepted this ruling and Boobyer, who naturally lost the hole and the match 2 and 1, accepted his misfortune in a most sportsmanlike manner."

A more recent and even more unusual rules problem arose in a Mixed foursome. The husband had driven just past the corner at the 1st hole. The wife thinking she might just reach the green with her very best shot, attacked the ball with a flurry, but did not disturb it — until, in returning the club to the start position, she knocked the ball back and it hopped over the cop into the practice ground. "What happened next"? as they say in *A Question of Sport*. Fortunately Roger Robinson, a member of the R & A Rules Committee, happened to be on the opposing team, and he supervised the replacement of the ball with a 1 stroke penalty. The ball was not out of bounds, as a backward movement of the club with no intention of hitting the ball is not deemed to be a shot!

Dr John Lawrie and Woodley Benson were very different golfing types — Woodley, a keen but indifferent performer and a typical club supporter, whilst John, a member of the R & A, had been a highly accomplished golfer.

The doctor had a severe speech impediment which didn't seem to embarrass him, despite being addressed as the inarticulate Lawrie on receiving his wand of office at the spring dinner in 1968. Around that time he was playing with the distinguished Irish international, Alan Humphreys, in the Easter foursomes and they had reached the semi-final. As Alan made his way to the first tee, the doctor beckoned him back. "It's in the b-b-b-b-bag" he said, to which Alan Humphreys slightly embarrassed replied, "I don't know about that. I think they are rather a good pair." "No, no", the doctor went on "you b-b-b-blithering idiot, I mean the b-b-b-b-b-booze."

Woodley Benson had joined from Wallasey. In those days club life was perhaps a little more formal than is presently the case and Woodley loved to tell the tale of how difficult it was to become accepted by the rather snooty RLGC members and how he frequently returned to Wallasey. "How's it going Woodley?" he would be asked. "Not very well; no one speaks to me" was the invariable answer. Several months later in the Wallasey clubhouse he was asked the usual question, but this time the reply was different. "I've had a break-through, one of the past captains spoke to me." "Oh good, what did he say?" "He shouted 'Fore'!"

Strange things happened to Woodley on the links. At the short 13th he was on the green for one and out of bounds for 4. He putted into a bunker, failed to get out with his first and thinned the next over the fence.

One winter's evening the talk turned to marriage. The young men sat round the clubroom in respectful silence as their elders ruminated. Woodley Benson small, but bright as a button, had, rather unusually, contributed little to the discussion. Eventually he piped up "I don't know what you fellows are talking about, I'm not only the most happily married man in the Golf Club, but I reckon I'm the most happily married man in the Wirral." Amidst manifestations of disbelief, Woodley was asked to justify his comments. "Easy", he said, "my wife lives in Hoylake and I live in New Brighton."

It must have been before this happy state of affairs that Mrs. Woodley Benson had rung the Golf Club to enquire about her husband's whereabouts. This was not an unreasonable request since it was six in the morning following the Spring Dinner. It may have been Read who answered the telephone "Just one moment Mrs Benson I will enquire." After a pause "Mrs. Benson, Mr. Benson left the club house half an hour ago with three other members. Shall I go after them? They can't have reached the fourth green yet."

Yes — it happened at Hoylake.

'HILBRE'

Epilogue

An epilogue is supposed to be the end of things. It may be the end of this anthology, but golf at Hoylake is still very much alive. The famous links are in good order now, but they have had their ups and downs. There have been times when greens and bunkers have been dappled with bare patches. On one occasion the course was so rough there was even a plea to bring back the rabbits to control the grass. Today under the admirable direction of our Links Manager, appropriately named Mr. Green, they are back to their best.

The view from the club room has not changed much in the last 100 years. There are a few more houses at the far end of Stanley Road, the gorse has thickened, but the rushes have mostly disappeared. The enduring vista of the dunes, the estuary and the Welsh hills set off by ever changing skies, sometimes an angry grey, sometimes a soft blue or best of all a gold and orange sunset, remains just as our forefathers have seen it. Doubtless the next generation will see the same. But sitting there in quiet contemplation one realizes that there are a few things that our forefathers have seen, which maybe the next generation will not see. Let's hope we are wrong.

In the previous pages the stories of most of our home-bred Hoylake champions have been told. There were others — an American Open Champion of 1924 Cyril Walker, who began his golf as a member of the Royal Liverpool Village Play Club. Two other Villagers, George Pulford and W.H. Davies, also distinguished themselves in the Professional ranks, but that is another story which hopefully will be told in detail in 1995 when the Village Play Club celebrates its centenary.

Will Hoylake produce any new Champions? The standard of golf remains high. We have 4 Scratch players amongst the men, and nearly 50 with a handicap of 5 or below. We can hold our own against the local clubs, whether it be the Men's Scratch team, the Colts or the Ladies, and we have cups in our display cabinet to prove it. Sadly however few now compete in the national Championships. Perhaps that says more about the Amateur Championships of today, than it says about Hoylake members. The Championships now have fields of youngsters with their starry eyes set on a professional career. Still let us hope that amongst our own enthusiastic Juniors, the 12- and 13-year-olds with their flowing swings, we have a Champion of tomorrow.

Will the next generation see another Open Championship at Hoylake? Whether they do nor not, our Honours Board in the Main Hall will continue to fill with great names and memorable occasions. We have the 1992 Curtis Cup and the 100th Amateur Championship in 1995 to look forward to; but when will we see the top professionals at Hoylake again? If they come, they will be hard-pressed to better the score of 64 set by Brian Waites in the third round of the 1981 European Open which stands as the course record. More than anything else we would like to see them here at Hoylake challenging for the Open Champion's Medal. To be realistic, however, the Open will have to change, or Hoylake will have to change. Maybe in years to come one will see a restriction on the number of spectators; or perhaps the wind and the tide will create some new holes for us out in the estuary, and so give us the extra space that is needed to enable Hoylake to stage an 11th Open Championship.

There is one more thing that our predecessors enjoyed. The Club had a reputation for its lunches, and particularly for the potted shrimps. Bernard Darwin in one of his articles about Hoylake, in *Out of the Rough,* finished with the words "Well, golf is a very good reason for going there, but let us not forget shrimps and friendship. These two, please heaven, shall still take us there, when I can only hobble, watching with a shooting-stick." We still have the friendship. Please may we have the shrimps again.

'ALPS'

Pen Pictures of Contributors

John Edward Behrend

John started his golfing career literally by accident. During his early school days, falls from a pony resulted in a broken arm and leg, which prompted his parents to ban riding until he had passed into Winchester. To provide a diversion, they gave him a few cut down golf clubs and and headed him towards Bromborough and Wirral Ladies, where his mother played. The diversion quickly became an addiction.

National Service followed Winchester and then Corpus Christi College Oxford for a degree in modern history. He missed his golf Blue, but won the Dinner Match and Captained the Divots. In 1959 the family Shipping firm of Bahr Behrend, which he had joined after graduating, posted him to London, a significant happening golfwise, for it gave him the opportunity to take lessons from John Jacobs who helped to develop his smooth rhythmic and highly effective swing. He soon became a formidable competitor. He joined Worplesdon, which led later to him being paired with the redoubtable Jessie Valentine in the Worplesdon Mixed Foursomes. They met for the first time on the tee — and won the event three years in succession.

John – The President's Putter, 1967

John had joined Hoylake in 1953. His return from London marked the opening of a golden era. He quickly established himself on the Cheshire scene, winning the County Foursomes four times, once with Bruce Thompson and twice with Peter Renison. He was runner-up in the 1971 County Championship and played about 40 times for Cheshire. He served on the County Golf Union Executive and became President in 1969. His deeds at Hoylake are legendary. He has won more than 30 Scratch medals, including the Club Championship three times, and has also had victories in the Easter, Summer, St. Andrews and Winter Foursomes. In 1976 Hoylake bestowed on him the ultimate

Club accolade, the Captaincy, at the comparatively youthful age of 42. He filled the office with distinction and, perhaps unexpectedly, enlivened many an Annual Dinner at local Clubs with the recitation of his whimsical golfing odes.

He has now reached the age of seniority (indeed he has just been elected a member of the Senior Golfers' Society) when many a golfer turns to Committee work. But he has already served 25 years in this sphere on Club, County and Royal and Ancient Committees. As a past member of the R and A Championship Committee, he has officiated at many important events. He figured in the celebrated ball-under-the-car incident in the 1979 Open at Lytham. Sevvy Ballesteros, edging into the lead in the final round, drove wildly 40 yards off line on the 16th. The ball finished under a car, on a part of the links designated for overspill parking. Ballesteros, the crowd and the world (via the attendant TV cameras) turned to the accompanying official, John E. Behrend, to await his ruling. He decreed that the Spaniard was entitled to "line of sight" relief and could drop clear. The rest is history. Ballesteros birdied the hole and went on to clinch the Championship.

John reached the pinnacle of his golfing career on the cold and bright morning of 18th September 1984 when he was summoned to drive from the first tee of the Old Course into the Captaincy of the Royal and Ancient Golf Club of St. Andrews. In the crowd were 30 Hoylake stalwarts who had travelled far to see their fellow member play the most important shot of his golfing life. The club rose, the cannon boomed its salute to the drive; but all was not well. John Behrend focused his attention on an unmoved ball. The gunner, his view obscured by the past Captains standing on the tee, had mistaken a practice swing for the real thing! A moment later all was well. With the fingers on the Clubhouse clock still indicating the appointed hour of eight, he swung smoothly into his shot, a controlled fade, to drive himself into the annals of golf and become the first local "son of Hoylake" to hold the revered office of Captain of the R and A. He achieved further notoriety that morning as the first Captain to drive in when not wearing a tie, a fact commented upon by the ever-vigilant Gerald Micklem. Taxed about his lapse, the new Captain pointed out reasonably: "I never wear a tie when I'm playing golf."

He has been a member of the Hittite Golfing Society for many years and became its Captain in 1974. He has won every one of its competitions at some time or another, including the Wooden Spoon! He Captained the Oxford and Cambridge Golfing Society in 1988 and 1989, and was runner-up in their President's Putter in 1967.

Nowadays the pace of his life has slackened somewhat. His enthusiasm for the game and his Club remains undiminished. He has had time to write a well-researched life of his hero *John Ball of Hoylake*. The limited numbered edition is a collector's item. He is a Trustee of the Royal Liverpool and is an enthusiastic curator of the Club's priceless treasures. He has a flat alongside the 2nd fairway with views across the Links to the Welsh hills — "inspiring but tempting a touch of head-up from the desk." As befits one who has played a leading role in encouraging the development of young golfers, he will quite often train his binoculars on some distant figure in the hope of spotting a latter-day Ball or Hilton. And there is nothing that would give him greater pleasure than to see such a one emerge.

Leslie Ernest Edwards

Leslie was born in Liverpool in 1906. He went to school in Wallasey. Following in his father's footsteps, he joined the *Liverpool Daily Post and Echo* and was soon reporting football matches which included such famous stars as Elisha Scott and Dixie Dean. He covered some of the great Open Golf Championships, such as Hagen's win at Hoylake in 1924 and Bobby Jones's at Lytham in 1926. He became Sports Editor of the *Liverpool Daily Post and Echo* for a number of years. He has been (and indeed still is) a first-class golfer, having played in many Amateur and English Close Championships, and was a member of Wallasey Golf Club for many years. He has been a member of the Royal and Ancient and the Royal Liverpool for some thirty years, and is a member of the Hittite Golfing Society. He is also a founder member, oldest inhabitant and honorary life member of the Association of Golf Writers. He has twice won the over-70 age group of the Senior Amateur Championship, once when he was 72, which included a round of 70 — two strokes better than his age! Leslie probably knows as much, if not more, than anyone else about twentieth century sporting events and personalities. He is a walking encyclopedia as he usually carries his filing system in his pockets.

Betty Lloyd

Betty has a very distinguished record in the world of Ladies golf. She was Cheshire Ladies Champion in 1951 and 1955 and was runner-up in 1950 and 1960. She was councillor on the English Ladies Golf Association in the years 1961 to 1964, its Chairman in 1964, and was twice Chairman of the Northern Division of the English Ladies Golf Association. As a young lady, in her twenties, she became Captain of the Prenton Ladies Golf Club in 1954 and Captain of Wirral Ladies Golf Club in 1957. She became the Cheshire County Golf Captain in 1968 and President in 1986 to 1987. At the present moment she is at work on a book to celebrate the Centenary of the Wirral Ladies Golf Club in 1994. She is also an architect, having graduated as Bachelor of Architecture in 1949, and a Deputy Chairman of the Wirral Bench since 1988, having been appointed as a Magistrate in 1970.

James Michael Marshall

Michael was born in 1919 and was educated at Radley and Pembroke College, Cambridge. During the war he fought in the Sudan, Eritrea, Abyssinia and up and down the Western Desert, where Rommel finally caught up with him. He was a prisoner of war for three years. During his confinement he passed his Law Society Final exams. He retired as senior partner of Bremner Sons and Corlett, a well-known firm of solicitors, in 1985 and more recently as Chairman of Grosvenor Developments Ltd. He was elected a member of the Club in 1937 and became Captain in 1960. His family has an honoured position in the Royal Liverpool as his father was Captain in 1934 and his son in 1989. Michael was the first Chairman of the Council and has been Chairman of the Green Committee on two different occasions. He is a Trustee of the Club, President of the Hittite Golfing Society and a member of the Senior Golfers' Society. His lowest handicap was 3. It is now 15, but he is still a dangerous opponent.

John Rees Roberts

John was born in Caernarvon in 1924 and is very proud of his Welsh parentage. He was educated at St.Asaph School and Liverpool University, where he graduated M.B.Ch.B in 1948 and became M.D. in 1958. He joined the R.N.V.R. from 1951 until 1973, became Surgeon Captain and, during this period, Queen's Honorary Physician, which was a great honour. He did postgraduate medicinal studies at London and Stockholm Universities 1954–58 and at Fullbright Scholar University of Cincinnati in 1956 when he met his lovely Swedish wife. They have three sons. He held the position of Consultant Paediatric Neurologist to the Liverpool Regional Hospital Board from 1960 to 1989. His golfing ability has not been quite as distinguished. His best handicap was eleven. For thirteen years he was a member of Formby. He is a member of the Royal and Ancient, the Senior Golfers' Society (now Secretary of the North West area) and the Royal Liverpool, where he became Captain in 1983, the year in which the Walker Cup was held at Hoylake. Although he describes his golf as indifferent, he has won seven Handicap Medal events. His main interests now are golf, fishing, reading and gin and tonics — not necessarily in that order.

Roger Tattersal Robinson

Roger was born at Hoylake in 1932, and educated at Westminster School, where he was a King's Scholar, and Trinity College, Oxford. After a number of years in the shipping business, he recently became Secretary of Eaton Golf Club near Chester. He has had a very distinguished golfing career having obtained an Oxford Blue, played for Cheshire frequently and won many Hoylake Medals. He has won the Hittite's John Ball Putter, has been runner-up in the Oxford and Cambridge Golfing Society's President's Putter and has reached the last sixteen of the Amateur Championship. Besides having been a scratch golfer he has been Captain of the Royal Liverpool and the Hittite Golfing Society and is a member of the Senior Golfers' Society. As a member of the Royal and Ancient he has served on many Committees including the Championship Committee, and the Rules of Golf Committee. He presently represents them on the Council of National Golf Unions and the Greenkeepers advisory body. His main dislikes are slow play and any breach of the etiquette of golf. If you are ever guilty of either of these offences, step well away from him.

John Ray Turner

John was born in 1916 and was educated at Chigwell. The Essex-based family road haulage business, which he joined on leaving school, became a subsidiary of Coast Lines during the 1930s. After the war he joined their head office in Liverpool, eventually becoming Chairman of the Company which in turn became a subsidiary of P & O. In his earlier days he attained a high standard in cricket at Club level, as well as playing golf for Essex. His lowest handicap was 1. When he emigrated to the Merseyside area, he joined Hoylake and was soon winning Medals and playing for the Club team. He became Captain in 1974. He is also a member of the Hittite Golfing Society and Senior Golfers' Society. His main interest now is visiting innumerable friends and relations which takes him all over England and to America. His favourite apéritif is a Dry Martini which is really a misnomer, as "not enough to charge for" is the Martini requirement.

Nicholas Curwen Williams

Nicko, as he is universally known, was born in 1940 and educated at Shrewsbury. His mother was a Hannay, a family which has had a long association with the Club. He is now the senior partner in a well-known firm of Liverpool stock-brokers. In his earlier days he played a great deal of cricket up to Minor County standard. Other activities include sailing and playing golf, at which he has had some successes, winning the Captain's Prize and the Summer Foursomes on several occasions. He is a great advocate of foursomes golf. He became Captain in 1988 and quickly earned the reputation of being a most amusing after dinner speaker. He is an ebullient character with a mischievous sense of fun. In 1965 he appeared before the Secretary for having broken the glass on John Ball's portrait, whilst playing golf up the stairs. He has now settled down a fraction and has a charming wife and two small children. It was his idea that this Anthology should be written — so it is Nicko you must blame.

Gordon Fotheringham Williamson

He was born in Wallasey in 1911 and was educated at Somerville School and Fettes College. From there he went into the grain trade for 46 years. He became President of the Corn Trade 1953/54 and President of the National Corn Trade Association 1962/64. He was an important member of the New Brighton Rugby Football Club, became Captain in 1934 and played three years for Cheshire in 1932/35. During the war he served with the 1st Battalion of the Liverpool Scottish (Camerons) and in the latter half of the war he was second in command of the 3rd Battalion of the Gold Coast Regiment in Burma. He became a member of the Royal Liverpool Golf Club in 1936 and was elected Captain in 1958, although as a player he never got out of his 'teens. He is affectionately known as "Poddy" which may possibly be due to the contours of his figure.